The Wisdom of Memoir

The Wisdom of Memoir

Reading and Writing Life's Sacred Texts

by
Peter Gilmour

With a Foreword by James Carroll

Saint Mary's Press
Christian Brothers Publications
Winona, Minnesota

Genuine recycled paper with 10% post-consumer waste.
Printed with soy-based ink.

The publishing team for this book included Carl Koch, development editor;
Jacqueline M. Captain, manuscript editor; Amy Schlumpf Manion and Barbara
Sirovatka, typesetters; Maurine R. Twait, art director and cover designer; cover illustration by Joy Wallace; pre-press, printing, and binding by the graphics
division of Saint Mary's Press.

The acknowledgments continue on page 180.

Printed in the United States of America

Printing: 9 8 7 6 5 4 3 2 1

Year: 2005 04 03 02 01 00 99 98 97

ISBN 0-88489-427-4

Library of Congress Catalog Card Number: 96-71340

Contents

To my dad,

John B. Gilmour

Foreword

"We all live in the past," G. K. Chesterton wrote, "because there is nothing else to live in. To live in the present is like proposing to sit on a pin."

We move forward by looking back. We know where we are going by studying where we have been. We steer by instincts learned in a lifetime. In this way, each pinpoint of the present, while entirely new, takes on the meaning of what precedes it. Intelligence, feeling, imagination, and even conscience are all functions, first, of memory.

Memory is the human faculty that gives shape to experience. Memory provides the narrative structure by which we uncover meaning. Memory is the source of knowledge, understanding, and wisdom. Memory imparts compassion. Instead of sitting on a pin, through memory we sit on a vast, commodious plain, at home with our truest selves, and with all other creatures both past and—here is the wonder, for memory generates future too—those to come. Memory makes visible what is otherwise unseen. Thus memory is the fountain of biblical belief, for, as the form of the Scriptures themselves attest, God leaves traces in history that can be recognized as such only after the fact.

All of this is why the literary form of memoir is precious, and why Peter Gilmour's reflection on it is important. In this book, the common human impulse to bring the past into the present is affirmed both as art and as spirituality. Mr. Gilmour draws on the masters of the genre to show how every person is a memoirist. And he demonstrates with rare clarity how, through memoir, the intensely private becomes an act of public generosity. Thus memoir is both an antidote to loneliness, and the occasion of community.

Peter Gilmour brings unique insight, especially to the contemporary forms of this ancient enterprise, showing why more and more writers have turned to memoir; and why modern readers are properly consoled by it. *The Wisdom of Memoir* is a user's guide, a manual, a commentary, a shrewd literary analysis, a deep reflection, and a stirring celebration of a sacred and saving impulse.

JAMES CARROLL
Boston, Massachusetts

Author's Acknowledgments

Researching and writing about memoir, its wisdom, and its theology makes me wonderfully aware of the interrelatedness of the stories of our lives and the lives of our stories.

I thank personalities in my intellectual genealogy: Timothy E. O'Connell, John Sprague, and Carl Koch. Tim, as the director of the Institute of Pastoral Studies (IPS) at Loyola University of Chicago, first encouraged me to research memoir as a form of narrative theology. John, as the editor of the *Critic,* first gave me a forum to publish reflections on memoirs, some of which are included in this book. Carl, as an editor at Saint Mary's Press, in addition to seeking out this book for publication, offered many perceptive suggestions that strengthened the manuscript. Likewise, I am grateful to Loyola University of Chicago for a funded research leave in 1995, which made the completion of this book possible.

Other Loyola benefactors include the Institute of Pastoral Studies' students, especially those who participated in my course Autobiography and Memoir in Religion. IPS graduates Kathy Heskin and Terry Zawacki provided advice and encouragement, as did IPS computer consultant Howard Lintz. As well I applaud my colleagues who actively encouraged this project by being available for consultation, by reading drafts of the manuscript, and, thankfully, by offering constructive criticisms: Camilla Burns, SND; Tad and Noreen Monroe Guzie; Patricia O'Connell Killen; Mary Sharon Riley, rc; Stephen Schmidt; William Schmidt; and the late William G. Thompson, SJ. Other faculty members' presence aided this project: James Armstrong; John Buscemi; Kathleen Dolphin, PBVM; Richard Woods, OP; and James R. Zullo, FSC. Graduate assistants Kate Kinser and Elizabeth Mazur cheerfully and effectively helped with the many and varied tasks of book creation. The staff of the Cudahy Memorial Library at Loyola University of Chicago, especially Mary Donnelly, was always helpful in my quest for books and information.

9

Writers Marshall Cook, Ruth Creighton, H. J. Duffy, Rita Hansen, and Felicia Antonelli Holton offered valued professional advice as the manuscript neared completion.

The gracious hospitality of the monks of Saint Benedict Abbey, Benet Lake, Wisconsin, and Abbot Leo M. Ryska, OSB, who gave me use of the abbey's library, have not gone without appreciation. I thank them, as well as other people who extended hospitality as this manuscript developed: Donald Cunningham, SJ; Michael McGinniss, FSC; Patrick and Elizabeth O'Brien; and Joseph Rost.

I am grateful to all my neighbors and friends in Wisconsin whose curiosity about and interest in this writing project was always supportive and inspirational, especially Ron and Dorothy Van Maldegiam; Joy Wallace and David Gilbertson, resident artists of Camp Lake whose work beautifies the world; their daughter, Leah; Jay and Val Krasne; John Dumke; Linda Paulsen; and the Johnson and Povlsen families.

I have not forgotten good friends in Chicago, especially Patricia Campion; John Conroy; Patricia Dodson; Joseph and Jeanne Foley; Gerry Fross; Gary and Patti Joyce; Mary Kincaid; Marty Laub; Jerry O'Leary, OP; Stephen and Myrel Titra; and Gordon Will. I thank them for allowing me to be absent in their lives as I wrote this book.

Nor have I forgotten other friends from near and far: Helen and Jamie Doherty of Christchurch, New Zealand; Joy and Jim Reisinger of Sparta, Wisconsin; Gus and Sandy Ripa of Bethlehem, Pennsylvania; David Robertson of Eugene, Oregon; Joseph Roccasalvo of New York City; and Robert J. Smith, FSC, of Winona, Minnesota. They too, thankfully, are ever present.

Introduction

This Thing Called Memoir

It had been some years since he last attended this convention. Delighted to see him once again and looking forward to renewing acquaintances, I took the seat next to him at one of the sessions. We were listening to a paper on chronic illness. This paper, written by a scholar who himself is chronically ill, merged highly personal experiences and insights with professional theory and analysis. As the presentation continued, my associate, long absent from such proceedings, penned this short note to me, "Is it the fashion now to speak so personally in these papers?" Not wanting to miss one word of this engaging paper, I simply wrote "Yes!" on the bottom of the note and returned it to him.

Later, over dinner in the hotel restaurant, the two of us expanded our truncated correspondence into trumpeted conversation. He was surprised by the turn that academic research had taken and fascinated by the tone it now embodied. The authority of abstraction, the preference for the propositional, the truth of the theoretical—the more usual characteristics of academia—had new, perhaps rival, company: colorful, descriptive, specific, concrete, artistic, and distinctly subjective narratives of personal experience. He found this turn of events intriguing and told me, "Such an approach might make the results of research more interesting and hopefully more accessible to wider audiences."

Taught by My Students

My own fascination with memoir has its roots in a course that I teach, ambitiously titled, Religion, Storytelling, and Literature, in the Institute of Pastoral Studies at Loyola University of Chicago. This course initially focused on four distinct story types: children's stories, stories from religious traditions, life stories, and the stories of contemporary novels.

Each time I taught the course, I became more and more impressed with the particular and peculiar power that life stories possess.

Memoirs energized course participants in unique ways. I noticed how these life stories functioned as guides, leading course participants into new and different worlds. I observed how memoirs acted as mirrors in which readers saw reflections of their own life stories. I listened to my students speak of the spiritual qualities of certain secular memoirs. They brought other memoirs that touched their heart to my attention. Ted Long, for example, introduced me to Jill Ker Conway's *The Road from Coorain,* a memoir of her Australian childhood and adolescence.[1] Myrel Cooke insisted I read *The Last Farmer,* Howard Kohn's memoir of his Michigan farm family.[2] And Randy Gibbons loaned me her copy of Lillian Schlissel's *Women's Diaries of the Westward Journey.*[3]

Through these and other students' enthusiasm, I became increasingly conscious of stories from life and their unique ability to illuminate life's mysteries and bespeak of the presence of the holy. Following the example of my students, I found myself also energized to linger longingly and lovingly over memoir. Eventually the fascination with memoir became so great that I created a separate course, Autobiography and Memoir in Religion, which gave me even greater opportunity to delve into these manifestations of life events and experiences.

Memoir, Memoir Everywhere

Memoir transcends the college classroom. It has evolved into a major form of communication. I come across and hear about these stories in a variety of places and from a wide cross section of people. I came across Tim McLaurin's memoir of boyhood wellness and adult illness, *Keeper of the Moon,*[4] while strolling through the Southern Festival of Books in Nashville, Tennessee, with Bob and Mary Lou O'Gorman. John Sprague, when he was the editor of the *Critic,* sent me a copy of Heinz Kuehn's memoir, *Mixed Blessings,*[5] which records and reflects on Kuehn's coming of age in Nazi Germany. Onetime neighbors and all-time good friends Dennis and Liz Keenan brought Kathleen Norris's book *Dakota: A Spiritual Geography*[6] to my attention.

Even a casual browser in today's bookstores or a cursory reader of weekend newspapers' book review sections notice the myriad of memoirs now published. Some are scams, sensationalized pulp, not worth money or time. But many other memoirs are deeply reflective stories that capture and communicate portions of the inestimable mysteries of life and living. I found Brent Staples's memoir, *Parallel Time*,[7] while browsing in a bookstore on the south side of Chicago. Doris Grumbach's memoir, *Extra Innings*,[8] waited patiently for me to discover it at the Barnes and Noble Bookstore in Evanston, Illinois. And, fortunately, Jill Ker Conway's second memoir, *True North*,[9] was available for purchase in a bookstore in the Atlanta airport when I was caught between flights.

Real World Stories for Real World People

I call the style of knowledge and expression that surprised and fascinated my colleague, that energizes my students, and that has grown into a significant story style for the contemporary world, memoir. I define memoir as a narrative that captures and communicates one's own specific life experience and its individual and social, personal and communal significance. Since the author of a memoir is its subject, and the subject of memoir is its author, such a narrative focuses, deepens, and, in some cases, even creates identity.

This process of creating memoir is an essentially spiritual activity because it centers on how one chooses to be human, what it means to be human, and what finally are the implications of such a humanity. The product of creating memoir is an artistic combination of memory, reflection, and imagination, and this product manifests spirituality. I like to think of spirituality as a constellation of particular attitudes and practices that undergird a conscious and continuing process by which a person discovers, rediscovers, focuses, and deepens what ultimately is important to him or her. Memoir as a manifestation of spirituality creates, as we shall later explore, icons of experience.

Dimensions of Memoir

On the surface, memoir may sound individualistic and egocentric, but an in-depth look at this style of knowledge and expression reveals otherwise. Memoir embodies extraordinarily social dimensions. A well-reflected-upon story of personal life experience reveals other socially significant stories. Brent Staples's *Parallel Time*, for example, not only relates his personal story as an African American, but also captures and communicates the social reality of racial prejudice.

The phrase *socially significant stories* includes stories from religious traditions. Commenting on the contemporary significance of the classical storyteller from religious traditions, Elie Wiesel writes, "The legends he brings back to us are the very ones we are living today."[10] The stories of our lives illuminate significant stories from religious traditions, too. The title of Nancy Mairs' memoir, *Ordinary Time,*[11] captures the connection between life events and religious tradition. The phrase *ordinary time* indicates the mundane, but it also indicates the holy in its echo of the segment of the church's liturgical year known as Ordinary Time. This memoir, like its title suggests, weaves together contemporary experience and religious tradition into a single cloth.

Of course memoir presumes serious and substantial reflection on life and living. If, as Socrates said, the unexamined life is not worth living, then, through memoir, as the late Fulton J. Sheen said, life is worth living. The encounter with other people's memoirs moves us to see and examine our own life more distinctly and clearly. Constructing one's own memoir supplies both an occasion and a methodology for significant reflection.

One's own constructed memoir is also an exercise in generativity and communicability. Other people, those who are near and dear to us, those totally unknown to us, and those not yet born, are the potential beneficiaries of our memoirs. Ideally, memoir, in addition to being generative, is an exercise in effective and engaging communication. Other people will clearly understand the heart and soul of the memoirist because the author has expressed himself or herself well.

Looking honestly and deeply into the experiences of one's life, discovering the individual and social dimensions of personal activities, sharing these stories and insights with others—these are components of spirituality. How a person goes about these processes, what models of spirituality one finds helpful, and how implicitly or explicitly religious those models are may differ widely. Yet, examining, reflecting on, and sharing one's life events and the significance of one's life events—that is, memoir—is intrinsic to all worthwhile spiritualities.

The Embrace of Memoir

Memoir cannot be contained or corralled into one or another subject area. It travels easily among disciplines, yet with purpose and resolve. It contributes significantly to many areas of knowledge.

For example, the discipline of history increasingly respects memoir as both a repository of history and a resource for historians. This has, in many cases, led to the re-evaluation of many "official" histories and the reinterpretation of some historical theories. In 1995, fifty years after the atomic bomb's first and only use in war, the motives, methodologies, and morality surrounding its use underwent close re-evaluation. The recollections and remembrances of scientists and victims, politicians and pilots, generals and foot soldiers played a key role in the re-evaluation. Isabel Allende's memoir, *Paula,* although it centers on the fatal illness of her adult daughter, also contains valuable historical revelation and insight into her native Chile during and after the presidency of her uncle, Salvador Allende.

In various forms of counseling and psychiatry, clients relate their version of life events, and, as a result of the therapeutic process, come to new, deeper, more worthwhile understandings of their past. Past events do not change. However, more focused recollections of past events, new interpretations of past events, and establishing new relationships with past events are all part of the therapeutic process.[12] In less formal, more group-oriented settings like Alcoholics Anonymous, other twelve-step programs, and self-help groups, the process is similar. People reflect on their experiences of life, either with the help of a therapist or within the context of a group, thus creating spoken memoirs.

Memoir also plays a significant role in education, particularly the education of adults. The life experiences of participants ideally are valued resources both in formal courses and in other educational programs oriented toward adults. Each adult's personal story, alongside the specific subject matter, becomes part of course or program content. The participants' experiences and the significance of these experiences—their memoirs—function as unique and highly respected sources of knowledge, at times as ballast to theory, at other times as critique of theory. By bringing experience to the enterprise, every participant in adult education functions at times as a teacher of the group.

Since many educational theorists no longer draw strict distinctions between adult education and education for younger people, methodologies that honor personal experience now influence all levels of education.[13] William Ayers' memoir, *To Teach: The Journey of a Teacher,*[14] demonstrates this reality with elementary school students.

In religion, memoir has played highly significant roles. Testimony, the act of recalling one's conversion or the presence of God in one's life, has long been part of some religious traditions. In sacramental religions, confession or reconciliation relies on recollection of difficult past experiences in order to facilitate forgiveness and healing. Lives of the saints and saintly lives have always carried great weight and strength in all religious traditions. Christian religious education, for example, employs stories of virtuous and saintly lives as both a valuable resource and as an effective methodology on equal footing with scriptural, liturgical, and doctrinal resources. Richard Rodriguez, in his memoir, *Days of Obligation*,[15] specifically offers religious imagery as a way to picture the future.

Christians who gather in small groups to search out relationships between faith and life, known as Base Communities, are yet another arena where memoir serves a central function. In these groups, people share their stories with one another as a way to recognize the presence of Christ in their individual lives and in their social and collective worlds. These groups, like twelve-step and self-help programs, often function therapeutically for participants. The belief in God's present revelation and the relevance of Jesus Christ's Gospel message bring people together in these groups to share their stories of life and living with one another.

Memoir as Common Ground

Memoir possesses diplomatic immunity. It is able to move freely from one subject area to another, to bring together disciplines isolated by the strong tradition of academic departments, and to create a common ground. That common ground increasingly is experience, both individual and personal, social and communal.

Experience is the progenitor of all religions. It is the foundation of all religious traditions. Experience also is the product of all religious traditions. It manifests faithful lives and lively faith. Memoir—experience captured, reflected upon, and communicated—has the potential to function as a linchpin for present and future worlds and their spiritualities.

Martin Kramer, editor of a book on the practice of biography and self-narrative, claims that such interest in what I call memoir is the result of both a renewed appreciation for narrative and a quest for a shared humanism: "As academic specialties narrow, the practice of biography and the interpretation of self-narrative constitute common ground, where scholars can conduct a dialogue in which no discipline enjoys a uniquely privileged position."[16]

A Metaphor for Memoir

This search for possible common ground leads me to identify an operative metaphor of memoir: memoir is an icon of experience. This metaphor focuses on the common ground of experience while at the same time suggests its sacred character. The word *icon* denotes sacredness; the word *experience* connotes secularity. This metaphor for memoir reflects what Philip Phenix terms the "sacred secular,"[17] ordinary experiences that reveal infinite depths of meaning.

The Wisdom of Memoir

Ultimately, the product of memoir is wisdom. I like to describe wisdom as profound insight into life, living, loving, death, and eternity. Though often elusive and enigmatic, wisdom is captured and communicated in a variety of crucibles. Contemporary secular memoir is one such crucible for wisdom. Another such crucible, the Wisdom Tradition of the Bible, shares many common characteristics with contemporary memoir.

I mention this reference point in the Scriptures with initial caution, but with ultimate conviction. My intention is not to baptize memoir by paralleling it to biblical texts. To do so would violate the very nature of the Wisdom Books of the Bible, a decidedly secular literature that found its way into both the Hebrew and Christian canons. Rather, I believe, the incorporation of Wisdom literature into the Scriptures recognizes the importance of secular writings as sacred texts. One challenge of today's world is to search out, identify, and promote such sacred, secular texts.

The Plan of This Book

This book develops, in the phrase made popular by Clifford Geertz, a "thick description" of memoir. The first part of this book contextualizes memoir in human experience and religious tradition. It does so by identifying the various and varied forms of memoir in the first chapter. The next chapter explores memoir's contribution and service to religious and spiritual traditions. Chapter 3 draws parallels between memoir and the Wisdom Tradition of the Bible. It then speaks specifically about memoir both as theological reflection and as theology.

The second part of this book centers on participatory dimensions of memoir. Just as reading memoirs and reading about memoirs help one to understand better this style of story, so too does the act of writing memoirs contribute to the ever expanding research focused on memoir. Chapter 4 investigates the internal dynamics of memoir. Chapter 5 focuses on how best to read memoirs and how to go about writing one's own memoirs. The last chapter introduces genealogy and the genogram as intergenerational tools instrumental to memoir creation. An epilogue offers some final thoughts on the wisdom of memoir and memoirs of wisdom. The book ends with an annotated bibliography.

Reflections on notable contemporary memoirs at the end of each chapter await readers. I have included passages from each of these selected memoirs for several reasons. These excerpts open windows onto the worlds of these memoirs. They reflect the intensity and the artistry of each author. These segments, I hope, will lead readers of this book to read these and other memoirs as primary texts.

These reflections, not idle interlocutions, remind both author and reader that the theory of memoir flows from the practice of memoir, that the artistic product of memoir grows from disciplined and serious processes, and that the spirituality of memoir flows from living life and reflecting on its meanings.

Finally, after the two reflections in each chapter, reflective exercises offer readers the chance to ponder parts of their own story and, perhaps, begin writing them. Like other students, participants in my course Autobiography and Memoir in Religion have some of the usual attitudes about writing. Many are hesitant. Some are fearful. A few are catatonic. I find that writing assignments focusing on memoir are among the most helpful in moving students from hesitancy to enthusiasm, from fright to confidence, from catatonia to activity.

A creative restlessness settles on many memoir readers that only gets calmed by writing memoir. Tapping into other people's memoirs for insight, for guidance, for inspiration begins the search for wisdom. It need not, indeed it should not, end there. No person need act as if all knowledge, insight, and wisdom reside outside herself or himself. Rather, learning to read one's own experiences, learning to search out significances in one's own life is intrinsic to memoir. Ultimately, learning to share one's own knowledge and wisdom through memoir is the apex of generative participation in memoir.

1

The Many Manifestations of Memoir

Introduction

Human expressions that recall, reflect upon, and interpret life's experiences are hallmarks of every age: ancient pictographs on cave walls in Lascaux, France; detailed etchings on Mayan monuments in Central America; commemorative quilts hand stitched in Appalachia. These and many other preliterate icons of experience give testimony to the universal instinct of peoples throughout time to record and memorialize their significant experiences.

This chapter focuses on a variety of expressions that reveal life experiences and reflect upon their significances. Some of these forms are elemental utterances unconsciously spoken; others are hastily spray-painted graffiti; still others are long and detailed texts. They all express experience through a variety of forms, and they reflect significance on some level. The varied expressions presented in this chapter are all related to memoir, some distantly, others more closely.

Many texts considered in this chapter do not fall into explicitly religious categories nor have many of these texts been created by people considered overtly religious. Rather, we hear the voices, some muffled, others clear, of an assortment of humanity: soldiers, explorers, homemakers, citizens, politicians, and naturalists. Examples of formally religious texts of church persons are also here. These, too, are important and significant, not because they were generated within church precincts, but because, like their secular counterparts, they are able to reveal something sacred.

The Etymology of Memoir

The word *memoir* comes from the French language. Occasionally the word was used in diplomatic circles to refer to official reports. The more common usage, according to the Oxford English Dictionary (OED), indicates, "a record of events, not purporting to be a complete history, but treating of such matters as come within the personal knowledge of the writer, or are obtained from certain particular sources of information."[1] The OED also gives another meaning: "a person's written account of incidents in his [or her] own life, of the persons whom he [or she] has known, and the transactions or movements in which he [or she] has been concerned; an autobiographical record."[2]

Memoir and Autobiography

Some people mistakenly think memoir is only a section of a complete life story, and that it is the autobiography that relates a life story, whole and entire. Even though autobiography connotes telling a complete life story, no such story can ever be told or written in its totality. Even the most detailed autobiography is, in reality, selected portions of a person's life, a memoir.

Contemporary author William Least Heat-Moon illustrates the impossibility of autobiographical completeness in his book *PrairyErth*.[3] He tells the story of overhearing a brother and sister arguing at a roadside eatery in Chase County, Kansas.

"What've you ever done with your life?" [she said.]

[Her brother responded,] *"There isn't enough time to tell you all I done in my life."*[4]

This brief oral skirmish led Heat-Moon to consider just how long it would take to tell the story of his own fifty-one years of life. The next morning he dictated sixty seconds of his life into a tape recorder, and then, using the tape as a guide, began to write about that one minute of his life.

He stopped after completing six pages. He had not finished his self-appointed task; rather, Heat-Moon realized he was far from concluding. He estimated it would take ten hours to retell one hour of life, a week to retell one day of life, and three hundred fifty years to retell his fifty-plus years of life.

Reflecting on this experience, Heat-Moon states the impossibility of writing autobiography: "While I may pass my life in continuity and completeness, I comprehend it only in discontinuous fragments; of the lives of people around me my understanding is utterly fractured and piecemeal: scraps, shavings, smithereens."[5]

Famed American Catholic church historian, the late John Tracy Ellis, makes the same claim, though citing different reasons, in his memoir, *Catholic Bishops*. He writes, "Every attempt at autobiography must necessarily be incomplete, since one cannot tell the whole story, and that for many reasons among which a lack of remembrance is often a prime factor, along with the practice of selection."[6] He cites the title of an English churchman's memoirs that captures this reality, *Not the Whole Truth*.[7]

Autobiography is best understood as memoir, not memoir as part of autobiography. Given the reality that no autobiography is omnibus, it is both healthy and helpful to look at what traditionally is called autobiography as one type of memoir, a "life memoir." This distinction is helpful because it does not relegate memoir to an incomplete, partial, or second-rate text compared with autobiography. It also demythologizes autobiography as complete and total. Autobiography can only feign completeness.

This distinction is also helpful for would-be writers of autobiography. One need not be unduly concerned about leaving something out, forgetting incidents, or including an array of insignificant miscellany in the name of completeness. An autobiography need not, indeed cannot, be complete.

Scam Memoir Versus Authentic Memoir

A cautionary distinction needs to be made between scam memoir and authentic memoir. Scam memoirs masquerade as worthwhile, in-depth reflections on life experiences and events. They often center on a person whose experiences are momentarily in the limelight. They are often written by someone else. "As told to" sometimes appears as part of the byline; other times the ghostwriter appears as a coauthor. Publishers of scam memoirs try to turn a mighty profit relying on the popularity of the person rather than on the integrity of the memoir.

Closely related to scam memoirs are books that detail the strangest experiences without much, if any, apparent reason or motivation other than to sell books. Michiko Kakutani's review of *Secret Life*,[8] by Michael Ryan, and *Dreaming*,[9] by Carolyn See, compares such books to talk show participants who manifest a sense of urgency in relating their experiences. Ryan's account of having sex with his dog, for example, although well written, has little if any merit in the eyes of this reviewer. Although the headline to these reviews reads, "Confession Is Good for the Soul and the Sale," the article suggests more sale than soul therein.[10]

Such books demean the process of memoir and devalue its product. In theological terms a scam memoir is a sacrilege, the mistreatment of something sacred. Such aberrations of memoir should be labeled like cigarettes—SURGEON GENERAL WARNING: This product has been determined to be detrimental to your mental and spiritual health. Authentic memoir, by comparison, is a sacred activity that delves seriously and deeply into life's experiences and their significances. Authentic memoir, not scam memoir, is the exclusive focus of this discussion.

Repressed and Phantom Memory

More and more people today claim to remember experiences, usually traumatic, that they had forgotten. These people either remember what actually happened to them, usually after a long period of amnesia, or they create a "memory" of something that did not historically happen to them. Repressed and phantom memory are important and troubling contemporary phenomena that touch deeply on the authenticity, integrity, and spirituality of memoir. Other than to acknowledge the difficulty of determining which of these memories are historical and which are not, I do not consider such memoirs. At this writing, too many unanswered questions surround this phenomenon to include such rememberings—be they historical or fictive—here.

Forms of Memoir

Memoirs come in all shapes and sizes. The most obvious and prominent contemporary forms of memoir are book-length narratives, often subtitled "a memoir." Other related forms of memoir include diaries, journals, letters, commonplace books, confessions, manifestos, apologias, and even fiction. These varied forms of memoir capture and communicate experience and perspective on that experience. Some do this without the finely crafted artistry of a consciously revised and edited product. Others are carefully crafted, artistic icons of experience. The definition of memoir changes with each example. Predecessors to and variations of contemporary memoir reveal an intriguing fluidity.

Initial Stirring

Novelist and theologian Frederick Buechner, himself a memoirist of some distinction, terms forerunners of formal memoir in these words: *gutturals* and *sibilants*.[11] These groanings and gurglings, these hissings and hollerings, all spontaneously created without use of formal language, are primal expressions. More emotive and less communicative than a written memoir, they are nonetheless manifestations of the memoir instinct present in all humanity.

The exact origin of "Kilroy was here," an original graffito that first spread throughout the military during the Second World War, is unknown. Some researchers traced it to one person who first scrawled it on a bomb while loading it on the underside of a plane.[12] Though more understandable than the primal expressions of gutturals and jottings, it still does not communicate much reflection on the experience of Kilroy other than that he was at a given place.

This and other graffiti are testimonies to this basic instinct of humanity to express itself. People want to let others know about themselves, to create a record of their experience and its significance for others. Today's graffiti peppered on buildings and buses in urban areas, although considered by many to be ugly, unlawful, and too closely associated with gang and drug cultures, are contemporary testimonies to this same instinct.

It is interesting, insightful, and perhaps a bit frightening to realize that the early Christians used graffiti to identify themselves to fellow Christians and to remember and to express things important to them. The fish was a cryptic sign of a Christian. Another graffito, $\frac{P}{E}$, for these early Christians, signified Peter the Apostle. This marking was found during the twentieth-century excavations underneath Saint Peter's Basilica in Rome, thus giving more credence to the tradition that Saint Peter's in Vatican City is built over the grave of its namesake.[13]

Primal utterings, elemental statements, and spontaneous graffiti reveal the natural urge to signify that something has happened. Something had to be noted in the lives of people. Willy Loman's widow in the American drama *Death of a Salesman* captures this reality tragically, when she says:

> Willy Loman never made a lot of money. His name was never in the paper. He's not the finest character that ever lived. But he's a human being, and a terrible thing is happening to him. So attention must be paid. He's not to be allowed to fall into his grave like an old dog. Attention, attention must be finally paid to such a person.[14]

"Attention must be paid." These initial stirrings uttered and marked by people do pay attention to events and experiences. They are elemental and primal memoir.

Diaries

Usually constructed by daily dated entries, the diary is the most immediate record of one's experience. The diary, simply defined, is the creator's personal record. It is not written with the conscious intention that it will ever be read by others. Some diaries are made with a lock and key in order to promote privacy.

Samuel Pepys wrote the archetypal English diary. He was twenty-seven years old when he began the diary and thirty-six years old when he terminated the project. The first entry is dated 1 January 1660, the last entry dated 31 March 1669. During this span of years, the longest gap was one eleven-day silence. Pepys filled six leather-bound volumes and wrote in a shorthand developed by Thomas Shelton in 1626. He concealed erotic entries by using other languages in addition to cryptic abbreviations. His vivid descriptions, his eye for detail, and his astute observations about people give his diary a "You are there" quality.

What motivated Pepys to keep a diary is uncertain. He lived in interesting times to be sure. The changes in English government, the Plague of 1665, and the Great London Fire are a few of the events that he recorded. He was fastidious, exact, and exacting in living his life, which no doubt contributed to his motivation. "He may have been influenced, too, by the Puritan writers and preachers of his youth, who taught the value of a journal as a means of moral discipline. His diary bears traces of that influence in the monthly and annual reckonings in which he summarized the state of his affairs."[15]

In spite of the secret manner in which Pepys recorded parts of his diary and the fact that such diaries were not material for publication at that time, he did include his diaries in the impressive library that he amassed during his lifetime and bequeathed to Magdalene College. He stipulated that "[the library's] contents remain intact and unaltered."[16] Why such a precise personality included his diaries in this bequest if he did not intend them to be read is an interesting question, not just for students of Samuel Pepys, but for diary keepers in every time and place.

President Richard Nixon's close associate H. R. (Bob) Haldeman kept a diary during his White House years.[17] Published in 1995, after both Nixon and Haldeman had died, this diary contains more than six hundred pages in print. The complete version of twenty-two hundred pages, with movies, sound, photos, and related documents is available on CD-ROM. According to his longtime associate John Ehrlichman, Haldeman's diary does not capture "the setting, the sights, sound and smells of the places where the Nixon drama unfolded."[18]

This diary, short on interpretation, long on summation, does not offer much, if any, reflection on the significance of recorded events. Haldeman's purpose, apparently, was to create for himself a summation of daily activities. Had he, or anyone else who kept such a diary, chosen to write a subsequent memoir, the information within that diary would have been helpful.

A lesser-known, but nonetheless intriguing, diary in American religious history is the *Burtsell Diary*. Richard Burtsell was a priest of the archdiocese of New York. His diary, nearly five thousand pages in thirty-five ledger books kept from 1865 to 1912, chronicles a particularly intriguing time in American Catholic church history when Americanism and Modernism were significant ecclesial issues of the day.

Church historian John Tracy Ellis was the first to use the resources of this diary in his *Life of James Cardinal Gibbons*.[19] Subsequently Rev. Robert Trisco and Rev. Emmett Curran relied on the resource of the *Burtsell Diary*, but according to Nelson J. Callahan, a contemporary scholar of this diary, both men misrepresented the man behind the diary.

It is my thesis that the Burtsell Diary should be seen for what it is: the story of a gifted, obedient, and remarkably intelligent priest of the Archdiocese of New York who maintained a position of loyal opposition to what he felt was wrong with the direction of the

U.S. Church in his own lifetime and who, in many ways, would have been far more comfortable in the Church after Vatican II than he was in the Church of his own day.[20]

Diaries such as Burtsell's frequently present alternative views from what are often called "official" histories. The diaries are so much more than a "piece of positive data capable of being researched in an archive."[21]

Since the diary is primarily a personal document, it functions as a depository of recorded events for its author. It also functions as a place where one can pour out heart and soul. In this respect a diary frequently functions as a good friend, that is, a listening, nonjudgmental presence in the writer's life. As people reread their diaries, they are better able to recall and reflect on the experiences they have recorded.

Journals

Journals are slightly more formal than diaries. A journal is a record written with the intention of creating a usable reference. In contrast to diary keeping, the author of a journal writes with a more conscious purpose, usually to supply a written record, not only for oneself, but also for colleagues, for superiors, and ultimately for posterity. Some journals are kept because their job either demands the workers do so, or because the workers think that it is a good idea. Other journals are kept because the author feels involved in something that is or may be significant. Still other journals are kept to trace a predominant theme in one's life.

Two multivolume journals adorn American history and letters, the Lewis and Clark expedition journals and Henry David Thoreau's Walden journals. *The Journals of Lewis and Clark* record the daily activities and discoveries of the exploration of the Louisiana Purchase. The first entry, 13 May 1804, at the River Dubois opposite the mouth of the Missouri River, begins these chronicles of Lewis and Clark's more than two-year adventure; the last entry is dated 24 September 1806.

Each officer had orders to keep an individual daily record. Enlisted personnel were encouraged to keep journals of their own, and a few did so, producing documents that are today of great value when used together with the more ambitious journals of the two captains. The total disappearance of Robert Frazier's journal (after published copies had actually been advertised for sale) and the complete bowdlerizing of Patrick Gass's (through the revision of a well-meaning clergyman who had no appreciation of its frankness and earthy vigor) are regrettable losses.[22]

These journals are the records of the expedition of twenty-eight men through what eventually became ten of the United States. They were guided by a Shoshone Native American woman named Sacajawea, whose son was born on the expedition. This journey, grown to mythic proportions in national consciousness, is documented through these journals. A comparative reading of these journals not only reveals a wealth of information, but also a bit of plagiarism. At times Lewis is either copying from Clark's journal or vice versa. At least one of these two rugged adventurers and detailed journal writers occasionally slacked off and copied his partner's entry!

Henry David Thoreau's two-year, two-month stay (1845–1847) at Walden Pond on the outskirts of Concord, Massachusetts, is recorded in his extensive journals. One of the true classics in American literature, *Walden* is an artistic expression of Thoreau's time living alone at Walden Pond. He compresses his twenty-six months of experience into a single year and organizes the book by seasons. This artistic icon of his experiences, produced as a result of seven revisions, was finally published in 1854, some seven years after the experience. On the other hand, the actual journals of his time at Walden Pond are multivolume and provide a far more extensive, detailed record of this experience. They are "a kind of memory, in which thoughts were hived."[23]

One biographer of Thoreau, Robert D. Richardson Jr., notes Thoreau's interest in the 1632–1672 Quebec journals of *The Jesuit Relations*.[24] These journals comprise the annual reports of the Mission of New France from the superior of Quebec, Canada, to his Jesuit provincial in Paris, France. The form, a chronological journal, and the method, close observations and excursions, are similar to Thoreau's own journals.

In spite of Thoreau's careful, detailed, accurate journal entries, he felt something more was happening, something more was recorded. One of his journal entries reads:

There is no such thing as pure *objective* observation. Your observation, to be interesting, i.e., to be significant, must be *subjective*. The sum of what the writer of whatever class has to report

is simply some human experience, whether he be poet or phil-
osopher or man of science. The man of most science is the man
most alive, whose life is the greatest event. Senses that take cog-
nizance of outward things merely are of no avail. It matters not
where or how far you travel,—the farther commonly the worse,
—but how much alive you are.[25]

Thoreau anticipated the postmodern movement by more than a century. Ralph Waldo Emerson in his eulogy of Thoreau said, "He was a
born protestant."[26] By today's standard of postmodern thought, Thoreau's comments on subjective observation are more catholic.

Other journals document and decorate the experience of the
American landscape. Journals written by women during their westward journey in the nineteenth century are an important and unique
source of information. Although often referred to as diaries, these
writings were intended for others, and thus I include them in this section on journals. Some were written with the intention of being published in local newspapers back home. Others were constructed and
sent to relatives or friends planning on making the westward trek at a
later date. Lillian Schlissel's comparative study of hundreds of these
journals opens new windows on American history and American
women.[27]

The journal is a more public document than the diary. The author creates it with an audience in mind and with the intention of other people using it. Yet a journal is created at given moments, its
entries formed once and for all time. There is no rewriting or rework-
ing. The author of a journal intends it as a resource and guide for future use.

Letters

Letters can be broadly divided into two categories: (1) literary form
and (2) personal communication. Many epistles of the Christian Testament and Martin Luther King Jr.'s *Letter from a Birmingham City
Jail*,[28] for example, follow a literary form intended for large, public audiences. The second type, the letter for personal communication, is
the focus of this section.

Personal letters are yet another form of memoir. Usually intended
for a specific audience, often just one other person, letters are usually written for the moment. Yet some letters survive long periods of
time. Love letters particularly can be long-lived, so too can letters

written from front lines in war. Some families pass along letters from generation to generation.

For example, in my own family, letters survive from Civil War participants, some who fought for the Union and others who fought for the Confederacy. One particularly poignant letter is a brief memoir of my great, great, great uncle's death in Wisconsin. It was written by his widow to her parents in Virginia.

> It is with a sorrowfull heart that I seat my self to inform you of the death of my dear husband he was taken sick on the first day of this month and died on the third he ate his dinner as well as usual and about two o'clock he was taken with a violent pain in his side we had the doctor within a few minutes and he done every thing he could for him but nothing seemed to do him any good and then he called in another doctor they could not get anything to pass his bowels from the time he was taken he died about three o'clock the third day making only two days that he was sick he was sensible to the last minute he was very willing to die he took each of his children and kissed them and talked to them one by one he said he was sorry to leave us but we must try and do the best we could the preacher came to see him and talked with him and he was surprised to here him talk as he did he shook hands with all the men he had working for him and talked to them I think he hurt himself by working so hard and strong to get along and then when he got so he might have made some thing and then was taken away.[29]

Not encumbered with contemporary styles of punctuation, in several hundred words, the writer of this letter vividly recalls and interpret's her husband's last days.

Thomas Jefferson, realizing the importance of letters, used a device he called a polygraph to make copies of letters. He considered it one of the finest inventions of his era. Visitors to Monticello can see a polygraph on his desk in his study. By today's standards the polygraph looks primitive; by standards of his day, it is ingenious. In addition to accurate record keeping, this invention probably developed because people realized that many letters were significant documents detailing both personal and communal events.

Today the telephone, the ease and speed of transportation, the general decline in writing ability, and in some countries the unreliability of the postal system have all contributed to the demise of letter writing as a vehicle of communication. Whether or not fax machines hooked to phone wires and computer e-mail linked through satellite networks will bring a resurgence of narrative letter writing remains to be seen. Notes printed on fax or computer paper do not lend themselves to preservation the way a letter penned by hand on nicely designed stationary does. Words are there, but the visual effect of those words is often not particularly artful, stimulating, or beautiful.

Stanislas de Quercize, CEO and president of Montblanc North America, purveyors of exclusive and expensive fountain pens, claims that "the computer has devalued written communication. It doesn't fit the soul. To express a thought requires time. A fountain pen slows the pace allowing more time to think."[30] Even though de Quercize, I believe, unfairly demeans computers while promoting his own product, he does make a valuable point—"to express a thought requires time." Time fosters and facilitates reflection on experience.

Personal letters, like journals, are usually written without benefit of rewriting or editing. Many times the author sends the one and only copy of a letter. The recipient of the letter ordinarily decides whether it should be saved or tossed. Letters often permanently leave the hands of their authors.

Commonplace Books

Commonplace books are not so common today. Developed in England in the 1700s, the commonplace book was a vehicle for a person to collect significant quotes, passages, or sayings of other people. "It's a way of writing your autobiography using someone else's words," claims William Least Heat-Moon who, in his 1992 book, *PrairyErth,* begins each of the fourteen sections with "From the Commonplace Book," a series of relevant selected quotes from a variety of sources.

> After you get a book of these, if you gather them over a lifetime, you can look back and say, "This is what I thought was important when I was twenty. God, *now* look at what I think is important! Look what I thought was well written then and what I think is well written now." It really reveals ourselves to ourselves. But we just don't do it that much anymore.[31]

Even though most people do not keep meticulous commonplace books, many people informally collect quotes, sayings, or articles in some fashion. They might be found stashed in a favorite book, attached to refrigerator doors with magnets, stuck under the glass of a desk or tabletop, tossed into a drawer, or stored in a computer file. Some people have a favorite saying artfully rendered by a calligrapher. Others purchase posters of favorite sayings. Whatever the methodology of collection, haphazard or highly organized, such activity reflects commonplace book activity.

William J. Bennett's 1993 *The Book of Virtues* is a commonplace book on moral education.[32] Myriad quotes and excerpts are organized into ten categories: self-discipline, compassion, responsibility, friendship, work, courage, perseverance, honesty, loyalty, and faith. This book, rather than being individual in nature and orientation, has a social dimension and purpose to it. Bennett offers this commonplace book to improve the moral consciousness and spirit of the United States. And although Bennett himself is identified with right-wing Republicanism, and he developed this book when he was seriously mentioned as a presidential contender, *The Book of Virtues* is surprisingly void of his own personal political agenda.

Another book that makes use of the commonplace book tradition is Bruce Chatwin's *The Songlines*,[33] in which Chatwin writes about his personal encounter with the Australian Aboriginal people. Between chapters 30 and 31, Chatwin includes a section entitled "From the Notebooks." Some chapters subsequent to this section also contain commonplace book entries. He begins chapter 31 by making reference to his collected notebooks and one particular passage in his notebooks.

> In one of my earlier notebooks I made painstaking copies from Sir George Grey's *Journal,* written in the 1830s. Grey was perhaps the first white explorer to understand that, despite occasional discomforts, the Aboriginals "lived well."
>
> The best passage in the *Journal* is a description of a Blackfellow straining all his physical and mental faculties to stalk and spear a kangaroo.
>
> The last paragraph winds into a coda:
>
> . . . his graceful movement, cautious advance, the air of quietude and repose which pervade his frame when his prey is alarmed, all involuntarily call forth your imagination and compel you to murmur to yourself, "How beautiful! How very beautiful!"[34]

Grey's journal entry from the 1830s, recorded by Bruce Chatwin as a commonplace book entry nearly a hundred and fifty years later, motivates Chatwin to go on a hunt with Aboriginals.

Parts of the Hebrew Scriptures also have a commonplace book quality to them. The Book of Proverbs, for example, is a collection of aphorisms, maxims, and adages. So, too, does the Book of Ecclesiasticus, also known as Ben Sirach, collect many wise sayings. Often short and to the point, these biblical passages capture and communicate the practical wisdom of their day.

Keepers of commonplace books use other people's words to capture and express what is important to them. Certain quotations touch the hearts of some people so deeply that they create a record for their own edification and future reference. A commonplace book becomes "a spiritual sourcebook" for an individual just as the Bible is a spiritual sourcebook "for the civilization it serves."[35] Keeping a commonplace book is dependent, of course, upon a person who reads, a person who relates what is read to life, and a person who desires to create an archive of significant passages.

Manifestos and Apologias

Manifestos and apologias are two other forms of memoir. One contemporary memoirist, Paul Monette, claims that every memoir is a kind of manifesto. Defined as a public declaration of intentions, motives, or views, a manifesto has polemical and political intentions and overtones. There is little subtlety in a manifesto. The *apologia,* the term is Latin for justification, offers a defense for certain actions. The most famous religious apology, John Henry Cardinal Newman's *Apologia Pro Vita Sua,* gives a riveting defense of his move from the Anglican community to the Roman community of Catholicism.[36]

Some manifestos and apologias are heavy-handed, at times manipulative, texts. Others are more subtle and user-friendly, and state their case respecting the reader's intelligence and sensitivity. Regardless of style, they, too, are related to memoir. The common bloodline—personalized narrative that captures and communicates life experience and the significance of life experience—is indeed present in these texts.

Fiction

Another form of memoir, both intriguing and problematic, is the fictive memoir. In his biography of Jean Genet, Edmund White refers to this phenomenon as "auto-fiction."[37] Morris Dickstein defines auto-fiction as "edited memories that consciously blur the line between invention and recollection, novel and memoir, story and inventory. The stories have the slightly shapeless quality of real life and the haphazard way we tend to remember it."[38]

At first glance such concepts seem like contradictions. Memoir is supposedly factual, so how can a memoir be fictive? It is possible because the form that it takes can be imaginative without violating truthfulness. The truth of a story does not necessarily totally rest with its correspondence to factual events. Reality can be communicated through highly imaginative stories. Thus, some short stories and novels have memoir qualities to them, and some memoirs may have qualities of the short story or novel to them.

Nineteenth-century English writer Charles Dickens begins *David Copperfield,* a novel, sounding decidedly like memoir, "Whether I shall turn out to be the hero of my own life, or whether that station will be held by anybody else, these pages must show."[39] Another novel, *The Catcher in the Rye,* written more than a half century later by J. D. Salinger, makes reference to Dickens's famous beginning.

> If you really want to hear about it, the first thing you'll probably want to know is where I was born, and what my lousy childhood was like, and how my parents were occupied and all before they had me, and all that David Copperfield kind of crap, but I don't feel like going into it, if you want to know the truth."[40]

This work of fiction also rings of memoir.

Nobel Prize in Literature recipient Toni Morrison wrote her novel *Beloved* as a fictive memoir of a former slave and her family.[41] It intertwines stories of slavery and stories of slavery's aftermath. Morrison, familiar with slave narratives, knew these texts were politically motivated, that is, written to help bring about slavery's abolition. What Morrison calls "the . . . interior life"[42] was not revealed in these slave narratives. Yet Morrison wanted to get at the interior life in her fiction, and she accomplishes this through what she refers to as "literary archeology."[43]

There are two elements to literary archeology: (1) one's own life experiences, what Morrison terms "memories within," and (2) "the act of the imagination."[44] Memories within enable one to reflect on personal life experiences in order to gain insight into the memories within those who have gone before us. The other element, far more significant and important for Morrison, is the act of the imagination. This element gives her more "total access to the unwritten interior life of . . . people."[45]

Commenting on her work in a talk on memoir while she was in the process of writing *Beloved,* Morrison shed further light on the relationship between memoir and fiction when she said, "The crucial distinction for me is not the difference between fact and fiction, but the distinction between fact and truth. Because facts can exist without human intelligence, but truth cannot."[46]

This distinction between fact and truth imbues all artistic expression, but in memoir it becomes a particularly sensitive and important arena. Because the memoirist owns the experience, the reflection on the experience, and the narration of that experience, the author is thrice involved. Narration of experience almost always leads to questions about the relationship between design and reality. In memoir, the reflective process is added, and the relationship between design and reality raises even more questions, as has been pointed out by Toni Morrison.

Roy Pascal, through his groundbreaking work in the late 1950s, moved the understanding of experience and fictive expressions of experience toward a helpful symbiosis. As John Pilling has pointed out, "[Pascal] was intent on asserting that truth might partake of design and that design might embody truth."[47] Growing recognition of this relationship by subsequent critics and commentators has led to various other descriptions of the fictive dimension of memoir: for example, "versions of the self," "metaphors of self," "the art of life," "the voice within," and "autobiographical acts."[48]

Conclusion

The many and varied forms of expression, from gutturals, sibilants, and graffiti to biographies, manifestos, and fictive texts reflect, in varying degree, humanity's irresistible and unsatiated urge for expression and meaning. This is the genesis of theological reflection. People everywhere tell their own stories, expressing what proximately and ultimately is important to them. Then other people listen to or read these stories, however briefly or lengthily expressed, and this helps to establish and clarify meaning in their own life.

These expressions reveal, at least in part, what it means to be human. And through such revelations, the sacred nature of life and living begins to be manifested. These manifestations of the sacred, at times primal, emotive, and unrefined, at other times studied, disciplined, and sophisticated, are variant forms of sacred texts.

Elie Wiesel, a concentration camp survivor, a 1986 Nobel Peace Prize winner, and a writer of fiction and nonfiction, in his memoir, *All Rivers Run to the Sea,* remarks:

> "Memoirs?" people ask. "What's the hurry? Why don't you wait awhile?" It puzzles me. Wait for what? And for how long? I fail to see what age has to do with memory. I am sixty-six years old, and I belong to a generation obsessed by a thirst to retain and transmit everything. For no other has the commandment *Zachor*—"Remember!"—had such meaning.[49]

Contemporary memoir is both born and borne by this "thirst to retain and transmit everything." It is this urge that leads us to discover God, the presence of God, and the mystery of God.

This form of revelation—memoir—is distinctly of the real world, the stuff of profane daily life. It does not, at first glance, ring with religiosity. But these texts are sacred in their secularity. These human expressions, crucibles of wisdom, are icons of experience.

"The Road from Coorain": A Reflection

Americans "discovered" Australia in the 1980s. The shrinking purchasing power of the American dollar in Europe coupled with fear of terrorism prompted travelers to look for other shores to visit. The 1983 TV miniseries *The Thornbirds* and the 1986 film *Crocodile Dundee* stimulated the American imagination, if not with factual images of Australia, at least with sensational ones. Australia is a love affair for the traveling public: the famed Sydney Opera House perched on one of the world's most magnificent harbors, Ayers Rock (now called by its aboriginal name, *Uluru*), the Great Barrier Reef, and Tasmania rank high as tourist destinations.

The Road from Coorain, by Jill Ker Conway (New York: Vintage Books, 1989), however, avoids the tourist route. More difficult and demanding terrain is traversed: the heart, the mind, and the spirit. Jill Ker Conway's own personal transformation of consciousness is inseparably interwoven with a growing consciousness of her native land, Australia. In her memoir, Conway carves out new understandings, both of her physical geography and of her spiritual geography. *The Road from Coorain* is memoir as revelation, and it is sacred in its secularity.

The physical geography centers on Coorain (an aboriginal word meaning "windy place"), the sheep station purchased by Conway's parents where the author spent her childhood. Coorain holds both the magnificence and the terror of the Australian land. Large beyond the experience of most American farmers, the eighteen thousand acres of Coorain has no surface water. The closest phone is seven miles away, the closest town seventy-five miles away.

> When my father left in the morning to work on the fences, or on one of the three bores that watered the sheep and cattle, my mother heard no human voice save the two children. There was no contact with another human being and the silence was so profound it pressed upon the eardrums. My father, being a westerner, born into that profound peace and silence, felt the need for it like an addiction to a powerful drug. Here, pressed into the earth by the weight of that enormous sky, there is real peace. To

those who know it, the annihilation of the self, subsumed into the vast emptiness of nature, is akin to a religious experience. We children grew up to know it and seek it as our father before us. What was social and sensory deprivation for the stranger was the earth and sky that made us what we were. For my mother, the emptiness was disorienting, and the loneliness and silence a daily torment of existential dread. (24–25)

Drought, however, was the ultimate terror. "We on Coorain waited for the rain which never came" (69). Five years without significant rainfall during Conway's childhood withered the land, killed the animals, and more. Her father, who had became one with the land, died. "To those who know it, the annihilation of the self, subsumed into the vast emptiness of nature, is akin to a religious experience" (25), Conway wrote, foreshadowing and explaining her father's death, which had overtones of suicide.

Her mother then left Coorain, taking Jill and her two brothers to live in Sydney. The author experienced new dimensions of Australian life there: formal schooling, employment, and confining stereotypes both of women and of Australia. The tragic death of her brother and her mother's continuing inability to fully appreciate her daughter's inner quest made these years in Sydney difficult.

The book's spiritual geography centers on the author's inner journey. Her keen powers of observation coupled with her questioning mind energize this dimension of the story. Her parents' surrender of their individual religions at marriage, he a Catholic, she an Anglican, in order to forge a unified family life, prompted Jill to reject religious stereotypes. Her largely self-directed education at Coorain, markedly different from her later formal schooling in Sydney, opened her eyes to the chasm between authentic education and hollow schooling. She rejected idyllic British pastoral poets, instead becoming infatuated with T. S. Eliot's *The Waste Land*,[50] "which was about a landscape I knew." Indeed, she describes the plains in lines Eliot could have used:

On the plains, the earth meets the sky in a sharp black line so regular that it seems as though drawn by a creator interested more in geometry than the hills and valleys of the Old Testament. Human purposes are dwarfed by such a blank horizon. When we see it from an island in a vast ocean we know we are resting in shelter. On the plains, the horizon is always with us and there is no retreating from it. Its blankness travels with our every step and waits for us at every point of the compass. Because we have very few reference points on the spare earth, we seem to creep over it, one tiny point of consciousness between the empty earth and the overarching sky. Because of the flatness, contrasts are in a strange scale. A scarlet sunset will highlight grey-yellow tussocks of grass as though they were trees. Thunderclouds will mount thousands of feet above one stunted tree in the foreground. A horseback rider on the horizon will seem to rise up and emerge from the clouds. While the patterns of the earth are in small scale, akin to complex needlepoint on a vast tapestry, the sky is all drama. Cumulus clouds pile up over the center of vast continental spaces, and the wind moves them at dramatic pace along the horizon or over our heads. The ever-present red dust of a dry earth hangs in the air and turns all the colors from yellow through orange and red to purple on and off as the clouds bend and refract the light. Sunrise and sunset make up in drama for the fact that there are so few songbirds in that part of the bush. At sunrise, great shafts of gold precede the baroque sunburst. At sunset, the cumulus ranges through the shades of a Turner seascape before the sun dives below the earth leaving no afterglow, but at the horizon, tongues of fire. (5)

Conway came to realize that Australia was its own nation, not a colony, and she, like Australia, no longer needed to be limited by other people's definitions and descriptions of what it meant to be female in Australia. "I was living with a tragic deterioration brought about because there was now no creative expression for this woman's talents" (195), she wrote describing her situation after completing university studies in Australia and before departing for America.

Conway concluded that the harsh side of the Australian landscape, especially images of drought, disproportionately dominate the emotional life of Australians.

I knew that somehow it had to do with our relationship to nature, and with the way in which the first settlers' encounter with this environment had formed the inner landscape of the mind, the unspoken, unanalyzed relationship to the order of creation which governs our psyches at the deepest level. Australians saw that relationship as cruel and harsh, and focused the mind's eye on the recurring droughts rather than the images of plenty I could recall from the rich seasons at Coorain. It startled me to realize that although I was now running the enterprise at Coorain to produce an income that was handsome by any but the most plutocratic standards, my emotional life was dominated by images of the great drought. I wished there were a clear way to understand the process by which a people's dominant myths and mental imagery took shape. (218–219)

As an inner journey of feminist Australian consciousness, this memoir illuminates a fascinating land, its people, and the relationship between geography and spirituality, between place and myth, between earth and faith. After walking the road from Coorain, the reader has a useful map for traveling one's own inner journey and a strong desire to take such a trip.

"Keeper of the Moon": A Reflection

Written when he was thirty-six, Tim McLaurin's memoir prompts an initial question: "Who is this upstart author?" Memoir, among other things, connotes wisdom borne of age. Memoir writer and novelist Frederick Buechner claims, "There is something a little geriatric about it, too—an old codger putting his affairs in order as the end approaches."[51]

It need not be so, however.

A third of the way through *Keeper of the Moon* (New York: W. W. Norton and Company, 1991), McLaurin reveals that he has been struck with multiple myeloma, a rare and often fatal form of cancer. This is one milepost that contextualizes his reflections. My premature, somewhat embarrassing, judgmental skepticism of this memoir quickly receded. This book heralds more than a wisdom borne only of age, more than a winsome glimpse into growing up in the South, more than nostalgia from a too-youthful writer.

> At thirty-six one has trouble imagining his demise when the sun is shining, children play, and birds sing, but in those muted hours between midnight and dawn, I realized how easy it would be to slip out of this life and into the realm from which no one has returned. I often wondered what education or truth could be found in a young father having cancer. (277)

Tim McLaurin did spend some pages recording his experience of illness, a lens through which he now saw life and living, but this memoir focuses on growing up and growing. His boyhood world, although it encompassed only about a twelve-mile radius, was filled with unusual animals, ubiquitous planets, and unique people.

He was especially attracted to snakes—rattlers and copperheads—all daily fare for this kid who often carried snakes with him, kept them in his car and in his home, a habit that lasted into adulthood: a loose snake slithered alongside his wife in bed one night. Pit bulls and cocks, lovingly raised to fight viciously, were the central participants in time-honored rituals of the author's world.

The planets, the stars, and especially the moon were other mainstays of Tim's boyhood world. An uncle's gift of a telescope impacted his nephew's life in several ways. The telescope provided Tim with entrée into the vast universe beyond his own home turf and gave him status and importance in the school community. It also supplied the title of this memoir:

> I had volunteered to bring the scope to school and help our class raise money. The moon was in the right phase, half full, her glow not so bright that it drowned all surface features, the night sky clear and cold and hinting of frost. The principal announced over the intercom that the star machine was set up outside, and a tentative few came first to trade a dime for a cool view of the sky. Word spread. That smooth, dim coin of light that everyone but hunters or lovers took for granted now loomed into focus as a craggy, gnarled world of dramatic brilliance and shadows. Suddenly, I had become the keeper of the moon, the kid who knew how to turn the knobs and gears that lowered the sky till you felt you could reach and cradle it in your palm. I knew the answers to both kid and adult questions—how far away was the moon, what was it made of, did stars really fall; simple fare for a fourth-grader who had read every book on astronomy in the school library. Over the next few years on clear nights a farmer returning late from the fields, a mother and child, might knock at our door and ask for a quick sight of the moon or stars. I would swell out my chest and rush to get my coat, already telling the visitor what planets were in the sky. (32)

Many people populated Tim's boyhood, beginning with stern, loving parents. His mother, a strict disciplinarian, punished her children by beating them with switches that the kids themselves had to cut when they had been caught doing anything wrong. Herself in tears, she hugged them dearly after each switching. His father, whose understanding of animals at times exceeded his abilities to relate to humans, was not above physically abusing his wife and children. And others —brothers and sisters, uncles and aunts, cousins, neighbors, friends— added to Tim's experience and understanding of human nature.

Organized religion centered around the two Baptist sects his family embraced: Primitive and Southern. Bible reading before bedtime was a family ritual, and his mother taught Bible school, but "[his] questions remained stronger than her explanations" (38). Later, before Tim and his friends were about to go off to marine boot camp, they went to see a local minister. This man of God read and prayed the Scriptures with them, and told them to come forward at next

Sunday's service. Tim went to the service but could not bring himself to go forward at the appointed moment. He was struck by the real life of the real people who populated the pews, and he decided that whatever the organized church offered these people, it was not for him. Instead, he walked the other way, outside the church, and found himself in his preferred sanctuary of nature.

Years later, when told by his doctor of his cancer, he again eschewed formal religion, instead finding strength reflective of his own lifestyle. "I decided in that first minute I would not face this disease in a passive mood, but would confront it as an intruder. I felt more pissed-off than afraid, more hassled than victimized" (275). He conquered cancer through six four-day treatments of chemotherapy, and then, a year later, through a bone marrow transplant that took him away from home for 101 days.

Throughout Tim McLaurin's memoir, two seemingly opposite forces form and reform his world. The first force is centrifugal, the dream to leave home, the drive to encounter new worlds, the desire to scope the stars. The second force is centripetal, the homing pigeon instinct, the return after traveling new worlds, the forever fascination with that plot of ground into which he was incarnated. The dynamic equilibrium of these two forces forged Tim McLaurin's spirituality, illuminating the people, places, and events of his still young life.

> We are sons and daughters of the land, our heritage tied to field and woods, the call of hunt, the spiritual transition of the seed that cracks the hard earth and grows into weed, food, flower, or tree. I have carried in my wallet for seven years a plastic sandwich bag filled with plain dirt scooped from the pasture behind the homeplace. It has traveled with me through Africa, Europe, and much of America, a talisman that whispers to me the song of mourning doves, wind in longleaf pines, the low rumble of thunder from a summer storm that has recently passed and soaked the dry fields. I hope to waltz slowly to that tune the day I lift above this bright land.
>
> I have told you of home. (316)

Tim McLaurin's cancer, a milepost in his thirty-sixth year of life, became an occasion for reflection on what his life, and all life, means. His memoir stretchs back to his earliest memories, another milepost, vividly recalling, relating, reflecting on them as a way of dealing with and destroying an early death call.

Reflective Exercises

❖ Do you know of any diaries or journals kept by present or previous generations of your family? What impressions do you have from reading such documents?

❖ Recall either receiving or writing significant letters. What did these letters say? How are they important for you now?

❖ What are some of your favorite proverbs or sayings? What sayings do you recall your parents or grandparents repeating to you as you grew up?

❖ Have you read any novels that were so real to you that they were like memoirs? What made them ring with reality?

❖ What influence does the landscape in which you grew up have on who you are?

❖ Did you ever move from one place to another? If so, how did this affect your life?

❖ When you were growing up, what was your favorite animal?

❖ Recall an incident from your childhood or youth when you were punished for doing something you weren't supposed to do. Who was there? What happened? As you look back, how did such punishment shape your character?

❖ What events and experiences of your life stand out as mileposts for you?

2

The Depth and Breadth of Memoir

Introduction

Memoir has interdisciplinary and social dimensions. Varieties of religious experiences and cultural traditions illustrate these dimensions of memoir. Memoirs, like icons, are created and developed by real people in real-life situations. They, like icons, bespeak of things sacred, and in turn become sacred things.

Whatever their style or form, authentic memoirs are icons of experience. This word *icon,* originally from the Greek, denotes image or portrait. The word also reverberates with both contemporary and classical connotations. Some contemporary usages of this word, regretfully, minimize and even rob it of its great heritage. The little symbols on the computer screen are often called icons. Some public personalities are called icons: for instance, Michael R. Milken was at one time referred to as an icon of Wall Street. Such usages devalue the original meaning of the word. The older, wiser meaning of the word suggests something sacred, artistic, and mysterious.

In the Byzantine tradition, especially in the Russian Orthodox church, an icon both captures and reflects the divine. It links earth to heaven. As an instrument of sacred communication, an icon is a door to heaven in the Byzantine tradition. These icons have been described as theology in color.

This appreciation and reverence for icons did not happen easily. The Iconoclastic Controversy, lasting well over a hundred years (726–843), struggled with the appropriateness of this artistic style. Ad-

44

vocates of icons saw them as intimately connected with the Incarnation. Since God had appeared physically in this world, it was right and proper to portray God in material form and to venerate this form. Icons continued this work of the Incarnation. Critics saw these artistic representations of the holy as a dangerous flirtation with material representation of the human figure and an idolatrous veneration of images. They smacked of secularity, a flirtation considered unworthy of and dangerous for any truly religious person. The iconoclasts wanted all icons destroyed, and set to the task. Fortunately, they were unsuccessful.

The Iconography of Memoir

The sacred texts of memoir are much like the history and tradition of icons. Building on the aforementioned description of icons as theology in color, memoir is theology in descriptive, specific, concrete, subjective, artistically constructed words. Like the classical visual icons of the Orthodox tradition, memoir as spiritual and religious expression is looked upon with suspicion and even hostility in some precincts. Memoirs are viewed as secular, not sacred, texts that glorify a faulty notion of the importance of the individual. To some, memoirs are occasions of sin.

Other people venerate memoir as an appropriate gateway to mystery, leading people toward the divine. For them, memoir reflects the Incarnation. Memoirs focus on the divine in the material world. By centering on the individual person's experiences, memoirs embody and reflect social memories and meanings. They are, therefore, sacred texts.

Social Dimensions of Memoir

Memoir echoes larger worlds. Every memoir reflects not only the individual but also the social, not only the personal but also the communal, not only the local but also the universal.[1] The famed Native American Sioux Holy Man Black Elk speaks of this reality in the opening lines of his often cited memoir.

> My friend, I'm going to tell you the story of my life, as you wish; and if it were only the story of my life I think I would not tell it; for what is one man that he should make much of his winters,

even when they bend him like a heavy snow? So many other men have lived and shall live that story, to be grass upon the hills.

It is the story of all life that is holy and is good to tell, and of us two-leggeds sharing in it with the four-leggeds and the wings of the air and all green things; for these are children of one mother and their father is one Spirit.[2]

Irish poet W. B. Yeats also captures this relationship between individual life and collective life in his life memoir. He writes, "All life weighed in the scales of my own life."[3] Black Elk stresses all life as the lens through which he sees his own life and life story; Yeats stresses his own life as the lens through which he sees all life. Both Black Elk and Yeats agree that a relationship exists between an individual life and the totality of life.

This relationship between individual and personal, social and communal life has been moved into even greater consciousness by Thomas Berry. He explores this relationship both by an expansive understanding of collective life and by an egalitarian placing of humanity within its context. First, Berry highlights the universe in its totality and complexity as the collective realm in which each individual person lives. Secondly, Berry does not give the human species dominance over this universe. Rather, he sees the universe as a communion of subjects, not as a collection of objects for people to use as they please. Some ancient and contemporary memoirs reflect this relational, nondominant consciousness and connection to the universe. Such memoirs reflect Berry's strongly held belief that "every living being of Earth is cousin to every other living being."[4]

Literature, whose early roots rest in the origins of myth, religion, and ritual, also reflects the reality of the social and communal in memoir. G. K. Chesterton reminds readers: "Every great literature has always been allegorical—allegorical of some view of the whole universe. The *Iliad* is only great because all life is a battle, the *Odyssey* because all life is a journey, and the Book of Job because all life is a riddle."[5] Memoir, where subject (the author) and object (the author's experiences) are one, also reflects this symbiosis, perhaps even more intensely than the classical myths do for many contemporary readers.

Ritualized memoirs are overtly communal, embodying the experiences of whole groups of people, and are authored collectively. The Jewish people during their Passover seders recall their collective memoir, the Exodus from Egypt as told in the Haggadah. They tell this story by ritually re-enacting their passage from slavery to freedom. The Triduum—Holy Thursday, Good Friday, and the Easter Vigil of Holy Week—is a communal Christian ritual memoir. During Holy Week, and more specifically, during the Easter Vigil, Christians tell a long version of their story. The nine readings, seven from the Hebrew Scriptures and two from the Christian Testament, begin with creation, move through the Exodus and the prophets, and conclude with Christ's Resurrection. Although often this lengthy series of readings is truncated in actual pastoral practice, the reading from Exodus is never omitted.

Preliterate societies focused their energies primarily on the collective nature and value of their stories. Their more public stories and myths—often in the form of poetry and drama—were memorized and performed for large numbers of people. These myths were forms of given peoples' collective memoirs.

Myths emphasize the collective over the individual and the fanciful over the factual. The heroes and heroines of myths are larger-than-life people, often descended from gods and goddesses, and therefore in closer contact and communication with the divinities. These characters and their experiences capture and communicate the origins and ideals of a people. Myths remember and reflect what makes a given group of people unique. Performances of myths were at times part of religious ritual. They are, then, fictive, collective memoirs.

Sacred Oral Customs of Memoir

In addition to myths, that is, public collective stories, a more individualized form of story transmission resided in the custom of telling one's stories of experience. Older tribal members would tell their life experiences to selected younger members. Older members of a culture passed on their spiritual wisdom to the next generation through these stories. Tellers of these stories knew they were participating in a sacred responsibility. Hearers of these stories sensed these recollections were privileged moments. These were sacred moments.

Such stories were not told to aggrandize the individual. Rather, they were told to strengthen the group. So strong was the recognition of the power that life stories contained that there were frequently taboos against tribal members telling these sacred life stories to outsiders. Black Elk, for example, violated this taboo when he told stories of his life to John Neihardt. To this day, some members of Black Elk's tribe feel that he should not have shared this privileged information with audiences outside of the Sioux nation. In a more recent memoir, *Neither Wolf nor Dog,* Dan, an elderly Native American, is careful to solicit the approval of tribal elders before he releases stories from his life to others outside the tribe.[6]

In Herman Hesse's great work *Magister Ludi,* also known as *The Glass Bead Game,* the story "The Rainmaker" vividly captures the process by which an older member of a tribe communicates the wisdom of his own life to three younger members. This process is no indiscriminate telling. It is contextualized in a master-disciple relationship. And often the number of hearers is limited to no more than three people. This intimate relationship adds both seriousness and sacredness to the process of communicating tribal wisdom. This is not a tribal media event.[7]

The Transition from Speaking to Writing

For millennia, the tellings of individual stories were, of course, oral events. The evolution of literacy did not necessarily extend the power and privilege of the written word to extraordinary numbers of people. That took time. Prior to the decline of the aristocracy and the rise of the individual, usually only people of privilege or wealth had the opportunity to write their own stories and to read other people's stories. Certainly Augustine, in his role as bishop of Hippo, was part of a privileged class that enabled him eventually to create his lengthy *Confessions.*[8] This life memoir was not widely available to masses of people for at least another thousand years. Books were scarce and expensive commodities, not only before the development of movable type in the thirteenth century, but for hundreds of years afterwards.

Illiteracy, the rule rather than the exception among common people, also prevented great numbers of people from having access to such works. Education among lower classes of stratified societies was rare until about three hundred years ago. In some places it was illegal to teach particular groups of people how to read and write. Such legislation in the United States kept almost all its slave population illiterate. Early efforts at universal education in Europe were often met initially with anxiety and hostility. Leaders who championed universal education—often motivated by religious charism, like Frenchman John Baptist de La Salle in the later part of the seventeenth century—

were often held in suspicion by the political, social, and ecclesial establishments.[9]

Christian Memoir

Early Christians, much like their pagan counterparts, knew that preservation and communication of their people's experiences were integral to their future. They remembered the names of their beloved dead at prayer. Local communities of faith developed lists of people important to their memory, and they kept the memories of these people alive by recalling various aspects of their lives, and at times, enlarging upon their lives imaginatively. At first these necrologies included little more than the death date, but eventually they evolved to include other biographical information and inspirational narrative.

Development of the Martyrology

The custom of local Christian communities keeping necrologies gradually evolved during the fifth century into the development of a universal catalog of saints. This listing, known as the *Martyrology,* was a collection of stories about saints' lives. Further developments of this text occurred, and, by the middle of the ninth century, the basic form of what is now referred to as the *Roman Martyrology* had evolved.[10] In 1583, Pope Gregory XIII promulgated this martyrology. Since then other popes have updated, altered, and edited the *Martyrology.*

Even though the *Martyrology* today suggests exclusive listings and lives of martyrs, other people were also included in these collections. Originally the word *martyr* meant witness. So people whose lives gave testimony to faith were included in the *Martyrology.* The term *confessor* was used to describe a person, not a martyr, who led a public Christian life. The names of virgins and widows were also contained within the *Martyrology.*

These treasured stories of local Christian communities collected in the *Martyrology* eventually became part of the Divine Office, the official prayer of the church. They were to be read at prime, one of the seven hours of prayer. Each day's entry concluded with the phrase, "and in other places, many other holy martyrs, confessors, and virgins." With this ritual the church recognizes that its official martyrology is an incomplete listing of saints. This concluding phrase of the ritual honors innumerable unnamed faithful and the importance of their unrecorded and unmentioned lives as significant in the story of the church.

Lives of the Saints

In addition to the *Roman Martyrology,* countless other collections of saints' stories flourished, especially during the late Middle Ages. The *Legendarium,* for example, was a collection of saints' lives developed in the late Middle Ages for use with common people. Perhaps the most famous collection of saints' lives is Alban Butler's *Lives of the Saints*. First published in 1756, Butler's *Lives* is a multivolume work that has been continually updated and is perennially available.[11]

In an age quite unlike the present, an age when literacy was limited and books scarce, when the opportunity to write one's own life was rare save for the occasional person of rank and privilege, the wisdom of people's lives was nonetheless preserved for posterity through biographical and inspirational stories. The Christian church became a memoir trustee for great numbers of people and, in doing so, created a body of communal memoir for its members.[12]

These Stories Today

These stories of saints and holy people mixed fact and fiction, but they testified to the importance of lived experiences. They were crucibles of wisdom, written by members of the church for other believing members. Edification of hearers and readers, not modern notions of historical accuracy, motivated their creation. Nevertheless, these sacred biographies are close relatives of contemporary memoir.

Since style of expression varied, dedication to historical fact differed, and ways to preserve and to access wisdom were limited, developing a contemporary understanding and appreciation of these collections of stories about saintly lives involves pastoral sensitivity and scholarly understanding. Hagiography, the study of saints' lives, can help the contemporary person to understand, appreciate, and mine these stories of heroes and heroines for wisdom. Hagiography is divided into two broad categories, practical and scientific.

Practical hagiography is essentially pastoral, developed at specific times and places for specific people. It aims to edify both believers and searchers through stories of the saints' faithful lives. The style of thought and theology of a given age, as well as the specific audiences for whom these stories were developed, give them a stylistic specificity that does not immediately transfer to other times and cultures. Many such stories thus need to be viewed through a prism of analysis in order to to be fully appreciated.

Scientific hagiography does just this. It offers a basically theoretical and critical study of this corpus of material. Much like contemporary biblical scholarship, scientific hagiography examines the social, political, and cultural contexts that produced these stories. It also pays close attention to the mores of literary genre and attempts to establish the intentionality of the author.

Scientific hagiography demonstrates the inappropriateness of treating these extraordinary stories as either biography or fiction. They are far too complex to be so categorized. Thomas J. Heffernan, in his study *Sacred Biography: Saints and Their Biographers in the Middle Ages,* hints at the complexity of these stories when he writes,

> The function of the text was not only to document the wondrous appearance of the divine in a woman or man, but also to interpret for the community what was only partially understood, mysteriously hidden in the well-known public record, and buried in the very ideal of sanctity itself.[13]

Hagiography and Contemporary Memoir

Hagiographical saints' lives and contemporary memoir are both different and similar. The most apparent difference is authorship. The stories of saintly lives were written by other people. In memoir the author is the subject. But a similarity also exists. Both subjects and authors of these stories of saintly lives share the common ground of a specific faith. Like contemporary memoir, they reflect the significance of the life written about.

Another difference occurs when comparing stylistic conventions of saintly lives and contemporary memoirs. Often the life of Christ provided the model, and even the rhetoric, to help the author of a saintly life communicate the significance of the person's story. By comparison, contemporary memoirs employ myriad styles to convey significance. Their often decidedly secular rhetoric does not presume or rely on a specific religious tradition to help communicate significance. These vastly different styles, however, are similar in their intentionality: to present life events and their significances.

To view these hagiographical texts then as collective memoirs is helpful from a theoretical point of view. The motivation for producing such documents, the reflective intrinsic qualities of these texts, and, at times, the artistry of the authors can be appreciated. Nonetheless, the imaginative, fanciful expressions of experience, the reliance on explicitly religious rhetoric, and the mystical and miraculous dimensions of hagiographical texts pose problems for many contemporary readers. From a pastoral point of view, these texts have lost their original vitality. In short, they are period pieces, able to be admired and appreciated through study and scholarship, but not particularly inspirational or moving for many people today.

The unfortunate emphasis on a factual interpretation of what today is recognized to be more fanciful expressions of faithful lives has soured many people who were exposed to these icons of the Christian story as part of their religious education. The emphasis on otherworldliness in these stories is out of vogue.

Another pastoral problem presented by these stories is that at times people gravitate to them as a way of avoiding or denying their present experience. Grasping such stories allows people to glorify the past, avoid the present, and ignore the future. Religion becomes a period piece, carefully controlled by a select group of stories, and usually immunized to God's ongoing revelation.

Testimonies and Confessions

Testimonies and confessions, two forms of memoir, like sacred biography, are explicitly religious in genesis and orientation. Their purpose is to evangelize hearers or readers into a specific community of faith, to further inspire the faith of existing members, and to reinforce the faith of doubtful or waning members. Thus the immediate purpose of testimony and confession is conversion, and the ultimate purpose is continuing transformation.

Testimony, long a tradition in certain Protestant communities, relates saving events personally experienced. Biblical language and religious rhetoric abound in Christian testimony. A distinctly predictable movement in almost all testimonies is well summed up by the lines of the song "Amazing Grace," "I once was lost, but now am found, was blind, but now I see." Testimony most often occurs within liturgical settings and therefore takes on aspects of ritual memoir.

One cannot mention confession as a memoir form without immediately thinking of the *Confessions of Saint Augustine*. No other Christian confession holds such a position of pre-eminence, though confessions in the Christian tradition are many. Augustine of Hippo penned this work between 397 and 401. Some consider it to be the first autobiography, a sixteen-hundred-year-old forerunner of the modern genre. Augustine related his past experiences in the light of his redemption through Christ. Over the centuries, Augustine's *Confessions* has become a standard by which confessions from other religious traditions are measured. The contemporary memoir *The Autobiography of Malcolm X* in part relates the author's Islamic experiences and has often been compared to Augustine's *Confessions*.[14]

Conclusion

The web of life works wonders. The most individual icon of experience is a prism of collectivity. No man or woman is an island, but rather, continuing with the words of John Donne, "every [person] is a piece of the continent, a part of the main."

Throughout history, various spiritual and cultural traditions have developed various methods to remember and communicate what they hold sacred. Recollection of lives and their significances are primary to all groups so that they might continue traditions identified as sacred and important to their histories. By doing so, various cultures and spiritual traditions extend their vision and influence to the present and into the future.

Contemporary memoir continues this tradition of memorializing lives and mining them for the sake of the commonweal. Even though many memoirs today stand outside any specific religious tradition, they are nonetheless spiritual because they portray the lived experience of the author's beliefs. Thus they function as sacred texts. In a postmodern age where expressly religious texts are increasingly under suspicion or perceived as irrelevant, expressions of the sacred that effectively communicate the divine dimensions of life and living need to be sought out, encouraged, and celebrated.

"Paula": A Reflection

Isabel Allende's memoir, *Paula* (San Francisco: HarperCollins, Publishers, 1994), illustrates well that memoir serves as a gateway to mystery, leading people toward the divine. Allende's memoir embodies and reflects social, familial, and communal memories and meanings. In so doing, it becomes a sacred text.

"My life is one of contrasts, I have learned to see both sides of the coin. At moments of greatest success, I do not lose sight of the pain awaiting me down the road, and when I am sunk in despair, I wait for the sun I know will rise farther along" (313). So writes Isabel Allende in *Paula*, which is named for her daughter. She penned this book at the bedside of Paula, first in a hospital in Madrid, Spain, and later in the author's own home in the Bay Area of California.

> When you wake up we will have months, maybe years to piece together the broken fragments of your past; better yet, we can invent memories that fit your fantasies. For the time being, I will tell you about myself and the other members of this family we both belong to, but don't ask me to be precise, because inevitably errors will creep in. I have forgotten a lot, and some of the facts are twisted. There are places, dates, and names I don't remember; on the other hand, I never forget a good story. Sitting here by your side, watching the screen with the luminous lines measuring your heartbeats, I try to use my grandmother's magic to communicate with you. If she were here she could carry my messages to you and help me hold you in this world. Have you begun some strange trek through the sand dunes of the unconscious? What good are all these words if you can't hear me? Or these pages you may never read? My life is created as I narrate, and my memory grows stronger with writing; what I do not put in words on a page will be erased by time. (8)

Isabel Allende is an internationally acclaimed novelist. Her first book, *The House of the Spirits*,[15] as well as subsequent novels, *Of Love and Shadows*,[16] *Eva Luna*,[17] and *The Infinite Plan*,[18] and a collection of short stories, *The Stories of Eva Luna*,[19] explore "both sides of the coin." The spiritual and the physical, the living and the dead, the rational and the transrational mystically meet and merge marvelously in her novels, and now, in this memoir.

Paula, in her late twenties, was living in Spain, and had recently married Ernesto when she was struck with the rare disease porphyria. She existed in a deep coma. Her mother was ever present in her daughter's lifeless life during this year-long ordeal. At the suggestion of her good friend and literary agent, Isabel Allende turned to writing as a way of enduring her vigil.

This memoir, like an intergenerational family reunion, reaches back to great-grandparents, grandparents, parents, and moves ahead to children and grandchildren. They are all present, the living and the dead, gathered together by Isabel Allende in memory and imagination. Together they cry and laugh, curse and pray, hate and love at the bedside of Paula.

The author is a niece of Salvador Allende, the first democratically elected Marxist leader in the Americas. His three-year presidency of Chile ended with the 1973 military takeover and his violent death. Isabel reflects:

Who was Salvador Allende? I don't really know, and it would be pretentious of me to offer a definitive portrait of him; it would take volumes, anyway, to describe his complex personality, the difficulty of his program, and the role he occupies in history. For years, I thought of him as just another uncle in a large family, the one representative of my father's side; it was only after his death and after leaving Chile that I became aware of his legendary dimensions. In private, he was a good friend to his friends and loyal to the point of imprudence; he could not conceive of betrayal and when he was betrayed found it nearly impossible to believe. I remember how quick he was with answers, and his sense of humor. He had been defeated in two campaigns but was still young when a journalist asked him what he would like to have engraved on his tombstone, and he replied instantly, *Here lies the future president of Chile.* In my view, his most outstanding characteristics were integrity, intuition, courage, and charisma: he followed his hunches, which rarely failed him, he did not turn away from risk, and he had the ability to captivate both masses and individuals. It was said that he could manipulate any situation to his advantage and that was why on the day of the coup the generals did not dare face him in person but chose to communicate by telephone and through messengers. He assumed the role of president with such dignity that it seemed arrogance; he had the bombastic gestures of a classical orator, and a characteristic way of walking with his chest out and holding himself very straight, almost on tiptoe, like a fighting cock. He slept very little at night, only three or four hours; you would see him at dawn reading or playing chess with his most faithful friends, but he could sleep for only a few minutes, usually in his automobile, and wake refreshed. He was a refined man, a lover of pedigreed dogs, objets d'art, elegant clothes, and strong women. He was very careful of his health, and prudent with food and alcohol. His enemies accused him of being a womanizer, and kept a close accounting of his bourgeois tastes, his lovers, his suede jackets, and silk neckties. Half the population feared he would lead the country into a Communist dictatorship and were ready to prevent that at any cost, while the other half celebrated the socialist experiment with murals of flowers and doves. (170–171)

The subsequent repressive actions of the military government—tortures, disappearances, murders—eventually forced Isabel and her family into exile. Her recollections and reflections on political exile paralleled her present personal state of affairs. Just as Paula seemed lifeless within her own body, so too did the spirit of Chile appear lifeless within its own borders during this rule of the military. And just as Isabel learned to live away from the country she loved, she now struggled with the distinct possibility of learning to live without her daughter.

After the coup, before her exile from Chile, Isabel Allende experienced a new Catholicism.

I became acquainted with a segment of the Catholic community that in a way reconciled me with the Church from which I had parted company fifteen years before. Until then I had known only dogma, rites, guilt, and sin, the Vatican, which ruled the fate of millions of faithful throughout the world, and the official Church, almost always the advocate of the powerful, despite its social encyclicals. I had vaguely heard of liberation theology and the movement of worker priests, but I knew nothing of the militant Church, the thousands and thousands of Christians dedicated to serving those most in need with humility and anonymity. They formed a part of the only organization with the ability to help the victimized, the Vicaría de la Solidaridad, an entity created for that purpose by the cardinal during the first days of the dictatorship. For seventeen years, a large group of priests and nuns would risk their lives to save others and to report crimes. It was a priest who showed me the safest routes to political asylum. (217–218)

Continually by the bedside of her daughter, Allende wrote her memories of life and living, bringing past generations into the present moment, bringing her beloved Chile and its upheaval into present consciousness, and bringing her own extraordinary life into perspective. Her childhood, her marriages, her love affairs, her writing, her friendship with Chile's Nobel laureate, Pablo Neruda, are but some of the author's many life events related and well reflected upon. She remembers for her inert, bedridden daughter, for herself, for her legion of legendary family members, both alive and dead, and, certainly, for readers who are also drawn close to Paula's bedside.

This memoir also captures the trials and traumas of family and friends who hover over a critically ill loved one in a hospital setting. The book explores what is presently happening; the solidarity developed with other patients, their family members and friends; the antiseptic and noisy nature of hospital routine punctuated by ever so brief appearances of specialists; and the ministering presence of nurses, the true healers of humanity, amid patients and visitors.

As the memoir moves through this agonizing, endless year, Isabel Allende, gradually and painfully, lets go of her highest hopes and dreams for her daughter, eventually accepts the inevitable, and ultimately turns death inside out. Death comes for Paula, but not like a thief in the night. Isabel Allende does not castigate her daughter's death as slave to fate, chance, kings, and desperados. Rather, through a mystical nocturnal visit from Paula, Isabel Allende fully realizes that now is time to let go, to encourage her daughter's departure, to help Paula continue her "strange trek through the sand dunes of the unconscious" to the other side where other family members stand ready to embrace her.

Near dawn on Sunday, December 6, after a miraculous night in which the veils that conceal reality were parted, Paula died. It was at four in the morning. Her life ended without struggle, anxiety, or pain; in her passing there was only the absolute peace and love of those of us who were with her. She died in my arms, surrounded by her family, the thoughts of those absent, and the spirits of her ancestors who had come to her aid. She died with the same perfect grace that characterized all the acts of her life. (325)

Life, like a coin, cannot have only one side. Death, like a coin, cannot have only one side. Isabel Allende marvelously, mysteriously, and mystically examines both sides of one coin in *Paula*.

"Days of Obligation": A Reflection

One contemporary memoir that continues the tradition of mining the experience of and meanings in people's lives for the sake of the larger community is *Days of Obligation,* by Richard Rodriguez (New York: Viking Press, 1992).

Long held as a concept that was the defining characteristic of the United States, the melting pot theory has itself melted down, and now has been remolded into a Rainbow Coalition of ethnic and linguistic multiculturalism. Some of the rhetoric raining from this newly fashioned consciousness forms a hodgepodge of political correctness, wish fulfillment, amnesia, and hallucination. Utterances by political prophets, gender gurus, and egocentric ethnics defy both the historical record and common sense.

Enter Richard Rodriguez. Uncomfortable with much of the contemporary rhetoric focused on identity, he raises his own voice in this picaresque memoir, *Days of Obligation.* He quickly takes on the word *Hispanic* as a bit of unacceptable rhetoric.

> Mexican Americans constituted the majority of the nation's Hispanic population. But Mexican Americans were in no position to define the latitude of the term "Hispanic"—the tumult of pigments and altars and memories there. "Hispanic" is not a racial or a cultural or a geographic or a linguistic or an economic description. "Hispanic" is a bureaucratic integer—a complete political fiction. How much does the Central American refugee have in common with the Mexican from Tijuana? What does the black Puerto Rican in New York have in common with the white Cuban in Miami? Those Mexican Americans who were in a position to speak for the group—whatever the group was—that is, those of us with access to microphones because of affirmative action, were not even able to account for our own success. Were we riding on some clement political tide? Or were we advancing on the backs of those we were drowning? (69–70)

After challenging the notion of "Hispanic," Rodriguez, a Californian by birth, a Mexican by heritage, probes the mysterious, changing identities both of Mexico and of the United States. He recalls that

California's history stands in marked contrast to the eastern shore of the United States where Protestant pilgrims viewed Indians as a hindrance to their work. The Spanish priests on the western shore of the continent, on the other hand, viewed the Indian as the occasion for their work. Today, the string of missions, the contemporary debate on the possible sanctity of their founder, Father Junipero Serra, even the ghastly and ghostly legend of the head of Joaquín Murrieta testify to an identity far different from the Pilgrims' saga.

Gold and manifest destiny eventually brought easterners westward. Anglo names—Sutter, Irvine—began to live alongside holy place names bestowed by Spanish missionaries. Eventually the Spanish holy place names were replaced by secularized Angloisms: "La Ciudad de Nuestra Señora la Reina de los Angeles de Porciuncula has become, in one hundred years, L.A." (122).

The Bay Area—San Francisco and its environs—is another focal point of Rodriguez's ponderings about a national identity. This city's onetime image, as "Land's end" (28), makes no sense now that the majority of its population have come over water from another direction, Asia. And the contemporary gay and lesbian lifestyle, gestated in San Francisco, has almost become a paradigm for a heterosexual lifestyle: two-career marriages, no children, conspicuous consumption.

One of Rodriguez's many vignettes hints at the complexity of contemporary identity: Mission San Jose. He deems it "a complete fake" (130), totally reconstructed in 1985, typified by a shirtless, sunglassed adolescent with skateboard who makes his way up the main aisle of the church: "He pauses with savage innocence and a certain grace" (132). Rodriguez asks if this would-be interloper is really an inheritor of authentic Californian identity who is practicing the (Holy) Days of Obligation?

No less ironic is Rodriguez's memory of his Mexican heritage. Survival is the primal and ongoing Mexican event. Originally misnamed "Indians" by the Spaniards, converted to Catholicism by missionaries, overrun by the Europeans, and robbed of land by the government of the United States, these people survived and continue to survive.

The joke is that Spain arrived with missionary zeal at the shores of contemplation. But Spain had no idea of the absorbent strength of Indian spirituality.

By the waters of baptism, the active European was entirely absorbed within the contemplation of the Indian. The faith that Europe imposed in the sixteenth century was, by virtue of the Guadalupe, embraced by the Indian. Catholicism has become an Indian religion. By the twenty-first century, the locus of the Catholic Church, by virtue of numbers, will be Latin America, by which time Catholicism itself will have assumed the aspect of the Virgin of Guadalupe.

Brown skin. (20)

Rodriguez counts himself as one of the benefactors of this legacy. He considers it an Indian achievement that he is alive, Catholic, speaks English, and is an American. Out of this identity he addresses the Catholic clergy on "multiculturalism" (194). He tells them at one point what they don't want to hear: have Latin masses. After the groans subside, he explains his thinking, not that of a disgruntled pre–Vatican Council II conservative frozen in the past, but an impassioned believer.

Fine, I say (Asshole) have your Spanish masses and your Vietnamese masses. But realize the Church is setting itself against inevitability; the inevitable Americanization of the grandchildren. You are going to lose the grandchildren; in fact, you've lost them already. You are papering your churches with poverty. You are using the poor to distract you from your failing enterprise. I'm beginning to suspect that you speak Spanish because in English you no longer believe. You are not feeding your lambs with Catholic assurances, you are feeding yourselves on the faith of immigrants. While second- and third-generation American Catholics go starving. A foreign-language liturgy should be a mere strategy, a temporary appeasement that should not distract us from our goal—the Catholic knowledge of union, the mystical body of Christ. We are Catholics, Fathers. We are Catholics living in America. But we are Catholics. (195–196)

In the introduction to *Days of Obligation,* Rodriguez writes, "In my mind, in my life, Mexico plays the tragic part; California plays the role of America's wild child" (xvi). But as the memoir progresses, these countries reverse identities. By book's end, tragic Mexico becomes comic and the comic United States becomes tragic. Tijuana and San Diego, exchanging forty million people annually at the San

Ysidro border crossing, become a symbol of this reversal, but it is also a new entity on the horizon. "Taken together as one, Tijuana and San Diego form the most fascinating new city in the world, a city of world-class irony" (106). A statistic—half of Mexico's population is under the age of fifteen—lends further credence to this reversal of national identities. Yet Rodriguez refuses to supplant one identity with another. "I believe the best resolution of the debate between comedy and tragedy is irresolution, since both sides can claim wisdom" (xviii).

Days of Obligation, a memoir that penetrates to bedrock, subtly asks the question, Why are so many United States citizens today gravitating to selective identities? The author challenges such behavior, suggesting that such people forget that America was formed in opposition to Europe. He both reinforces the contemporary urge to elect an identity and question the accuracy and integrity of some chosen identities. Rodriguez challenges readers not to ignore the witness of history, alter current reality, or skew the future in our individual and collective quest for identity.

"But I submit that America is not a tale for sentimentalists" (169).

Reflective Exercises

❖ Find some pictures of icons in a local library or visit a church or art museum with icon collections. What are the artists trying to embody and communicate through these icons?

❖ Recall powerful oral stories of life experiences you have heard family members or friends relate to you. What made them significant for you? Why do you think you recall them now?

❖ What saints' stories stand out for you? If your given name is a saint's name, can you recall the story of her or his life? Does it mean anything to you today?

❖ "I will tell you about myself and the other members of this family we both belong to," promises Isabel Allende. If you were writing your memoir, write a list of the members of your family that would have to be included as important to your story. Is there one tale about each that you would need to tell so that your reader would understand the importance of each one?

❖ Do you remember a key moment in your life when you felt a keener sense of your own family heritage? How would you compose the tale?

❖ Is there some incident in your own experience that stands out for you as an example of the complexity inherent in finding a national identity in the global village?

3

Memoir, Theological Reflection, and Theology

Introduction

The underlying perspective of the first section of this book is that secular memoir is sacred activity and expression. The Wisdom Tradition of the Scriptures provides a paradigm for understanding the place of contemporary secular memoir in theology and spirituality. Narrative serves as a form of knowing, and memoir emerges as a postmodern sacrament. Viewing narrative and memoir this way offers new perspectives on who is a theologian and what constitutes theology.

Explicit and Implicit Religious Memoirs

Although all authentic memoir is inherently sacred, some memoirs are overtly religious. *The Confessions of Saint Augustine* in Christian literature became both precursor and paradigm of expressly religious memoir.[1] *The Autobiography of Malcolm X* gives testimony to the power and persuasion of Islam.[2] Thomas Merton's *The Seven Storey Mountain* presents contemplative life to twentieth-century people.[3] Dorothy Day's *The Long Loneliness* prophetically calls Christians to practice—in addition to preaching—social justice.[4] And Kathleen Norris's *Dakota: A Spiritual Geography*[5] is, according to Patricia O'Connell Killen and John de Beer, an exquisite theological reflection on the geography and people of the western Dakotas. [It is an] insightful presentation of how religious traditions are shaped and shape communities and individuals. Norris' models draw on the sources of the Christian theological heritage to expand and deepen human experience.[6]

Many more memoirs are implicitly religious. They do not necessarily speak overtly of God, sin, grace, redemption, salvation, ecclesiology, moral living, and other theological realities, but they, nonetheless, are sacred texts. Writers of implicitly religious memoirs have the ability to recognize the sacred in the secular and to express it in ordinary, everyday terms. Jill Ker Conway's *The Road from Coorain* focuses on the geography of Australia both as revelation and symbol of life and living. Tim McLaurin's *Keeper of the Moon* turns to childhood memories as one way to explore meaning in a life-threatening illness. And Richard Rodriguez's *Days of Obligation* probes ethnicity and identity as gateways to understanding what life and collective life are all about.

Some readers easily see, appreciate, and understand secular memoirs as sacred texts. Other readers find this manifestation of the sacred through the secular difficult. Their criteria for what is sacred and for what is secular often predetermines their approach to and understanding of texts. Still other readers reject the possibility of the sacred expressed in and through the secular. They view everything secular as totally separate from the sacred, at least benignly godless or, at the extreme, the satanic enemy of the divine. They believe that only biblical words are precisely and exclusively God's word. Nothing more is called for, needed, appropriate, or true. This approach to the sacred exposes religion's Achilles' heel.

Religion's Achilles' Heel

Like all human enterprises, religion—meaning an organized body of believers most often centered around and manifested through church, synagogue, or mosque—is subject to institutionalization. A healthy organization degenerates into institutionalization when its original purpose is supplanted by the desire to preserve and protect its status quo at the expense of its mission. Once this happens to any organization, be it religious, governmental, or corporate, the essential goodness and enthusiastic spirit that motivated its origin and growth gets submerged and, in some instances, abandoned.

By my conscious and deliberate use of this term *institutionalization,* I intend to separate it both from the institution of religion and from religious institutions. Religion as institution is a mainstay of humanity, a permanent presence in life, and an abiding reminder of the often unseen, but ever real, divine realities. Described as such, the institution of religion is a positive and powerful force within the human enterprise. More specifically, religious institutions such as hospices, schools, and hospitals contribute vitally to the common good. Many citizens, religious and nonreligious, churchgoers and nonchurchgoers, have benefited greatly from the quality of schooling and healing such institutions offer. Some people commit their life and their career to making the institution of religion and religious institutions reflect divinity in the midst of this real world. None of these valued enterprises and treasured heritages are included in my use of the term, *institutionalization.*

Indeed, the institutionalization of religion is particularly insidious because the institution of religion and religious institutions can be strong forces of good. Religion, offering redemption and salvation, represents the most important realities in participants' lives. People who are charged with explicitly religious responsibilities, "the keepers of the Temple," possess significant stewardship. Their influence is strong both in the lives of people and in religion itself. When this sacred trust is violated, by those who keep the Temple, through deeds such as financial mismanagement or sexual impropriety, people feel especially betrayed.

Religion, like the pulls in Tim McLaurin's memoir, has both a centripetal and a centrifugal force. Ideally religion draws people into itself—its centripetal force—so as to be supportive and inspirational. Religion, at the same time, ideally, spins people outward—its centrifugal force—towards the sacrality of day-to-day events, experiences, and relationships. Religion becomes institutionalized when its own internal dynamics override its external mission. Parochial activity dominates at the expense of public presence. Institutionalized religion takes on characteristics of country club and cult.

Thomas Becket, as represented by T. S. Eliot in *Murder in the Cathedral,* refuses to allow the cathedral at Canterbury to become institutionalized.[7] The priests, who wish to preserve the status quo, lock the church doors, but Becket, dedicated to the true mission of church, says:

Unbar the doors! throw open the doors!
I will not have the house of prayer, the church of Christ,
The sanctuary, turned into a fortress.
The Church shall protect her own, in her own way,
    not as oak and stone; stone and oak decay,
Give no stay, but the Church shall endure.
The church shall be open, even to our enemies. Open the door![8]

Even at the expense of his own life, Becket deplores the institutionalization of church.

The Wisdom Tradition: Armor for the Achilles' Heel

So serious were the Hebrew people about keeping their religion healthily balanced that they incorporated texts into their canon of the Scriptures, the heart of their tradition, to remind them not to fall prey to religion's tendency to institutionalize and parochialize. These books, within the section of the Bible commonly known as "The Writings,"[9] act as ballast, preventing the priestly and the prophetic voices from scuttling the religious instincts of ordinary people.[10] The Christian Bible refers to them as the Wisdom Books: Job, Psalms, Proverbs, Ecclesiastes, the Song of Songs, the Book of Wisdom, and Ecclesiasticus, also known as Ben Sirach.[11] R. B. Y. Scott, one of the editors of the Anchor Bible series, refers to the voice of the Wisdom writings as a "third force."[12] This voice makes no appeal to the unique religious revelation of the Hebrew community as its source of authority. The voice of these wise people relies on a different source of authority: "The authority to which they chiefly appeal is the disciplined intelligence and moral experience of good [people]."[13]

The Hebrew religious traditions, theologies, and rhetorics are particularly and peculiarly absent in the books of "The Writings." Wise secular people took their position alongside other religious luminaries, the priests, and the prophets. They searched out the divine from different sources and expressed this Wisdom in other rhetorical forms. The presence of "The Writings" within the Hebrew canon of Scriptures and the Wisdom Tradition within the Christian canon of Scriptures make explicit that in day-to-day worlds the divine is manifested and that in day-to-day languages the divine ably communicates.

Contemporary memoir, like the canonical Wisdom writings, effectively embodies reflections on life and living in day-to-day language.

Theological terminology is eschewed in favor of the real-world descriptions and reflections on life experiences. Memoir moves its writers and readers deeply into the situation of life and real-life situations. Memoir moves people to consider this world's multitude of experiences and events as sacred.

Feminism and Memoir's Wisdom

The feminist movement draws inspiration from the biblical Wisdom literature that portrays God in feminine images. A woman of wisdom is a common image among feminist religious women.[14] This is no idiosyncratic occurrence. In some ways the feminist movement creates the same type of "third force" or ballast that the ancient Wisdom Tradition accomplished. Feminism did not come into contemporary religious thought through the religious tradition; it emerged into religious consciousness through the culture. Contemporary feminism is a good example of what Vincent Donovan, in his book *The Church in the Midst of Creation,* means when he says the culture must evangelize the church.[15] Contemporary feminism is in the process of doing just this: evangelizing the church.

Many recent books have explored the theory of writing women's life experiences. *Composing a Life,* by Mary Catherine Bateson, explores five women's lives as acts of creation.[16] Carolyn Heilbrun's book *Writing a Woman's Life* as well as *Telling Women's Lives: The New Biography,* by Linda Wagner-Martin, outline challenges and opportunities for women's memoirs.[17]

Among the many contemporary women who write life experiences, the four specifically singled out for extended reflection pieces in this book—Jill Ker Conway, Nancy Mairs, Doris Grumbach, and Isabel Allende—not only exemplify feminist theory but, through their work, have helped to identify, establish, and focus contemporary feminist memoir theory.

Reality Is Clearly Not What It Used to Be

Not only does contemporary secular memoir emulate the ancient Wisdom Tradition of the Scriptures, but it also embodies what has come to be called the postmodern paradigm. Memoir embodies a far different approach to reality than the styles of intellectual pursuit developed as a result of the scientific revolution and the Enlightenment. Significant personal and subjective forms of knowledge became devalued in a world enamored with science and rationality.

Only recently, under this marvelously intriguing yet amazingly ambiguous phrase *postmodernism,* have variant ways of organizing and expressing knowledge been given new hearings. Postmodernism heralds the breakdown of many prior absolutes. "Now the postmodern era is revealing a world in which different groups have different beliefs about belief itself," writes Walter Truett Anderson in his book *Reality Isn't What It Used to Be.*[18]

Pauline Marie Rosenau, writing the preface to *Post-Modernism and the Social Sciences,* points to the ultimate ramifications of this way of thinking:

> At stake are questions that pertain to the deepest dimensions of our being and humanity: how we know what we know, how we should think about individual endeavor and collective aspirations, whether progress is meaningful and how it should be sought. Post-modernism questions causality, determinism, egalitarianism, humanism, liberal democracy, necessity, objectivity, rationality, responsibility, and truth.[19]

I believe that the emergence of contemporary memoir as a way of knowing is but one manifestation and expression of this postmodern world.

Narrative, story contextualized in space and time, differs from abstraction, a theory universalized, which the scientific revolution and the Enlightenment championed. Narrative respects the voice of each individual by using the relationship between the author of the narrative and the subject of the narrative as a legitimate form of inquiry and expression of truth. Each person's unique relationship with reality leads to particularized knowledge and, when expressed, a singular voice.

To try to abstract truth from this relationship between people and their reality by identifying issues or formulating theories destroys the revelatory relationship of narrative, limits its subsequent expressions, and, although often unintentional, demeans individual persons. The recovery of narrative ways of knowing and communicating represents one of the revolutionary shifts in thinking that undergirds postmodernism. Contemporary memoir captures and reflects this shift.

The Wisdom Tradition Is Alive and Well

Like the biblical Wisdom Tradition, memoir provides ballast against the strong, destructive winds of institutionalization. Just as the Wisdom Tradition gave balance to the priestly and prophetic institutions of Judaism, memoir gives balance to the institution of the scientific and rational paradigm.

The contemporary world, long considered unfriendly toward religion, probably pales by comparison to the world in which the Hebrew people lived. Yet some of the texts of other peoples found their way into the Hebrew religious tradition both because they depicted the divine effectively and because they integrated the human into religion. Today, memoir offers religious traditions a path to reformation, away from institutionalization, toward authenticity and integrity.

The Abstract Mind and the Storytelling Person

The abstract mind, a product of the scientific and rational paradigm, works with issues and theories. In seeking to arrive at universal truths applicable in all situations, the abstract mind extricates issues and theories from experience. It treats their contexts ultimately as distracting flotsam and jetsam. The abstract mind stresses the objective, the theoretical, and the impersonal, but both the process and the product of the abstract mind is artificially and antiseptically limiting.

The narrative person, the storyteller, uses other ways and means to search out, state, and communicate reality. Narrative values experience as the heart of the matter. Flesh and blood, time and space are part and parcel of the narrator's approach to life and living. Memoir, rather than theory, becomes the narrator's receptacle for and reflection of reality. Narrative's characteristics—personal, subjective, grounded in the real world, specific—all are manifested in memoir.

Memoir as Narrative Theology

Narrative theology is "talking about God by telling stories of humans," according to contemporary Christian theologian Martin Marty.[20] When people tell their own stories they become authors of narrative theology. People become theologians when they tell their story or write their memoir, a particularized form of narrative theology. This is not an abstract, research-oriented mode of studying the holy, but a democratized, holistic, postmodern approach to knowing God.

While some theologians see memoir as an important source and manifestation of narrative theology, others view it as dangerous. On one end of the spectrum, Frederick Buechner, novelist and theologian, claims that "all theology, like all fiction, is at its heart autobiography, and that what a theologian is doing essentially is examining as honestly as he can the rough-and-tumble of his own experience with all its ups and downs, its mysteries and loose ends."[21]

On the other end of the spectrum is James W. McClendon Jr., who in *Biography as Theology* claims that autobiography is almost sure to be self-deceptive. Although he admits that the biographer can make mistakes, "only the *auto*biographer is virtually sure to produce a self-deceived account. . . . Proponents of truth via autobiographical self-display [are] adrift in a fog of subjectivity."[22]

I gravitate more toward Buechner's understanding of memoir as sacred story. Explicitly religious memoirs narrate the search for God overtly and employ theological language. An even larger body of implicitly religious memoirs do not specifically search for God, nor do they employ either abstract or denominational theological rhetoric. These narratives are not usually found in the religion section of a bookstore or library. Yet they represent an increasingly important and profound search for, location of, and articulation of the divine in life experience. They practice what twentieth-century theologians Paul Tillich, a Protestant, and Karl Rahner, a Roman Catholic, articulate in their theologies: the sacred is best manifested through ordinary life experience.

Memoir as Sacrament

As contemporary theology reasserts the tradition of understanding God's ongoing revelation in human experience, the reformulation of sacramentality is only to be expected. Outward signs of God's grace are sacraments, and these signs of God's grace may be and indeed are most commonly found in the ordinary experiences of human beings. The stories of these encounters are sacraments: actions of God.

Many people raised in sacramentally based religions have a static concept of sacraments; that is, they believe that the sacraments were instituted by Christ, that there are a specific number of sacraments, and that the sacraments have prescribed rituals. Of course, the historical record reflects quite another experience of sacraments. For instance, Edward Schillebeeckx in *Christ: The Sacrament of the Encounter with God* traces the pre-Christian origins of sacraments.[23] When life and religion were not so separately compartmentalized and before the refinement of the term "sacrament" that developed during the twelfth and thirteenth centuries, the church did not even quantify sacraments. The longer tradition in the church has been to look for signs of the sacred wherever they could be found.

Sacraments Frozen

Before the age of scholasticism—the eleventh century—sharp distinctions between sacrament and sacramental had not been constructed, nor had the number of sacraments been determined as precisely seven. In the Roman Catholic Tradition, sacraments became frozen within the seven specific forms only after the Middle Ages. When the Council of Trent gathered in the sixteenth century, it officially declared for the first time that the sacraments were limited to a precise seven. From then on, Catholics everywhere memorized, "A sacrament is an outward sign instituted by Christ to give grace." Catholics believed that only they could receive sacraments that left indelible marks on their immortal souls.

Between the time of the Protestant Reformation and Vatican Council II, one hint that sacraments might have a more embracing, far-reaching reality was found in the church's teaching about "sacramentals." But even sacramentals fell victim to hierarchical categories that had their origins in scholasticism and continued to exercise a heavy influence until the Second Vatican Council's *Constitution on the Sacred Liturgy (Sacrosanctum Concilium)* declared that sacramentals exist in order to sanctify almost every event in the lives of believers. This document underscores the church's deeply held conviction that all of creation can "be directed toward the sanctification of [people] and the praise of God."[24]

Sacraments Today

Sacramentality highlights a world charged with the presence of God, and sacraments function in this world. They, like memoir, are intimately and intrinsically connected to life and to life events. Rather than conceptualizing sacraments as things, Edward Schillebeeckx specifically defines Israel as a sacrament of God, and he describes the church as the sacrament of the Risen Christ.[25]

The various forms and styles by which many of the seven sacraments are now celebrated also contribute to a less object-oriented, more process-oriented, less individually oriented, more communally oriented understanding of what a sacrament is. Ideally, celebrations of sacraments are now riots of color, focused on the relational, better contextualized within specific communities, and indigenous to local cultures. In this way the celebration of sacraments parallels many characteristics of contemporary memoir.

Since Vatican Council II, Catholicism has moved away from an individualistic interpretation of sacraments toward a communal understanding of them. Sacraments, like memoir, embody, reflect, educate, and inspire communities of people. Such revitalization of the parochial practice of sacraments fosters a further understanding of the public reality of sacraments that embraces the world. Vincent Donovan, in his book *The Church in the Midst of Creation,* speaks of "sacraments for the world."[26] His less parochial, more public vision of sacraments poses a revolutionary question, "Is it possible that the true and ultimate meaning of the church, and the final meaning of the sacraments, can be found only *outside* the church, in the arena of the world, in the midst of creation?"[27]

The refounding of the church based on this question has left behind Euro-Catholicism as the single paradigm of Christianity and now embraces a true world church. Among the marks of such a world church is a sacramental vision less connected to parochialism and more connected to the world:

> What would all this mean for our understanding of the sacraments? The theology of the sacraments and the ministry of the sacraments would not revolve around deciding who has the power to administer them in the temple or the church or the sanctuary or at the altar, nor would it be about how much grace is accumulated by those allowed to receive them or about how many times they should receive them, nor even about the most effective liturgical manner in which to carry them out. Their ultimate meaning would lie not within the sign, not within the individual receiving them, not within the church—but outside, in the midst of human life. The most important ministry of the sacraments would be carried on out there, not around a temple or an altar.[28]

Memoir as a postmodern sacrament already has done what Donovan tells his readers, "It is time for us to leave our sacramental ghetto and to go out into our neighborhoods, our society, the world and help to restore our shattered community."[29]

This vision moves beyond parochial boundaries that limit sacraments to Catholics only and only as religious rites and ceremonies. Memoirs are sacraments of the postmodern world because they give signs of the sacred encountered in the world by ordinary human beings, not just by priests and prophets. The world is the recipient of these sacraments.

Theology, Theologians, and Theological Reflection

To search out the divine, to speak with authority on religion, and to relate the ideas of the holy to daily life and living, these have been the perennial responsibilities of theology, theologians, and theological reflection. Yet the postmodern paradigm asks anew: What is theology? Who is a theologian? And how does theological reflection happen?

A classical definition of theology, faith seeking understanding, has given way to a contemporary description of theology as a reflection on life. Many disciplines participate in reflection on life, among them psychology, sociology, anthropology, ecology, and philosophy. As people invest themselves in various subject areas and search out ways to communicate their insights that not only respect but also embrace holistic thought, new forms of scholarly discourse emerge.

One such form of reflecting on life, as ancient as people themselves, is, of course, narrative. Narrative's ability to embrace a wide range of knowledge coupled with its highly communicative nature and its celebration of subjectivity make it a language of choice for many contemporary theologians.

Theologian Patricia O'Connell Killen acknowledges the importance of people's stories in her work. She writes:

As a theologian, I have discovered the artful discipline of sitting with people's stories as a starting point for my reflection. I corral my own biases and splendid ideas, so that I might sit attentively, receptively, and nonintrusively until the stories' pattern, their central question, their heart emerges.

Only after my sitting bears fruit does my task as a theologian begin: describing the heart of the matter. I make explicit what is implicit, detail the significance of thoughts noted but not developed, and contextualize the powerful messages carried in these life experiences. I help name the questions and wonderments incarnated in lives before they can be spoken in words. As theologian I create the space for gracious and genuine conversation among these life stories of real people, the wisdom of the human sciences, and our religious traditions.[30]

Memoir accomplishes many of these same activities. Memoirists remember and reflect on experience; memoirists sit with stories and tell them in order to get to the heart of the matter.

Speaking of the Heart of the Matter

Narrative theology, talking about God by telling stories of humans, gets to the heart of the matter. And memoir, as one specific form of narrative theology, talks about God by telling stories of ourselves. Every authentic memoir is a form of narrative theology; every memoirist is a particular type of theologian. To deny memoir its participation in theology, to deny the memoirist her or his participation in theological reflection and, eventually, in theology itself, contributes to a patriarchal, exclusive, elitist definition and practice of theology that denies voice to and for all.

The minimal reliance on either denominational or professional theological vocabulary in this form of narrative theology makes memoir widely accessible to various publics. Novelist and theologian Frederick Buechner complains that too much theology is done in the mode of algebraic preaching or tourist preaching. While solving algebraic problems requires knowing at least one unknown, some theologians use language with all unknowns. Or some theologians are like tourists visiting countries that use languages other than their own. They raise their voices to obnoxious decibel levels and speak excruciatingly slowly, hoping that these behaviors will achieve communication. Neither algebraic nor tourist theology communicate. Memoir as theological expression avoids such aberrations.

James Hopewell says in his book *Congregation:* "The authority of Scripture, dogma, organization, and theological reasoning that once constituted the church, the *ekklesia,* has waned to the point of inconsequentiality for most Christians trying to make sense of their existence."[31] Memoir is one way to raise religious consciousness without relying on what many people feel is excessive and extraneous baggage from formal religious traditions.

Even for those people who find a particular religion or a given spiritual tradition inspirational and helpful in their life, there is almost no consensus, even within a specific religious tradition, about doctrine, authority, ethical behavior, or religious practice. Move outside a specific religious tradition to find common ground on creed, code, or cult, and divergence of opinion only increases. Such is the nature of life in a pluralistic world. Therefore common ground, both inside and outside of specific religious traditions, must be sought, lifted up, reflected upon, shared, and celebrated. The stories of memoir often provide such common ground.

Besides its accessibility to a wide variety of people, another hallmark of narrative theology is its public nature. Memoirs are published by respected commercial publishers and reviewed in the secular press. Many memoirs sell well, particularly when compared to theological books in the more classical, analytical style of academic discourse. Hence, in areas of the culture increasingly indifferent to or suspicious of the denominational and kerygmatic, memoirs have the capacity to relate to more people, some of whom might be associated with religion and some not.

The participatory nature of narrative theology is yet another of its important hallmarks. Its style invites emulation. Some people who come into contact with memoir will compose their own. These memoirs, in turn, will contribute to the ever growing corpus of narrative theology. Conceptual, categorical, abstract, and propositional theological texts seldom have such an effect on nonprofessional theologians.

Narrative theology, as embodied in memoir, has the ability to (1) give voice to people who have traditionally been voiceless in both culture and church, (2) communicate through language understandable to wider publics, (3) give people example and encouragement to tell their stories, and (4) reformulate the identity of theologians and reformat the definition of theology.

How Memoir Reflects

Memoir is particularly significant, and also challenging, to many models and methodologies of theological reflection as a process for reaching insight into life events for the purpose of guiding one's present and future behavior. The usually identified components of theological reflection are personal experience, culture, and religious tradition. Experience and culture are easily identifiable in memoir. As has been emphasized in previous chapters, memoir, as an icon of experience, has both individual and social, personal and communal dimensions. The most personal of stories, memoir, has cultural dimensions, just as the most cultural of stories, myth, has personal dimensions.

But what of religious tradition, the necessary third component to theological reflection? How specific, how focused, how explicitly "religious" need this aspect of theological reflection be? The paradigm of biblical Wisdom literature suggests significant human experience carefully reflected upon is a form of theology.

Roland E. Murphy, author of *The Tree of Life,* a book that explores biblical Wisdom literature, claims that "wisdom literature provides a biblical model for understanding divine revelation apart from the historical mode (salvation history) in which it is usually cast."[32] He goes on to say that human experience is one mode of dialog with divinity. This dialog with divinity, encapsulated in the Wisdom writings, allowed the Israelites to encounter their God "in a vital faith relationship that is as valid as the liturgical experience in the Temple, or the Exodus event itself."[33] Thus, Murphy places the revelatory nature of ordinary human experience as peer to both the extraordinary experiences of the Exodus and the Temple. Experience needs no better credentials.

Murphy then states what this model suggests for nonbiblical religions: "It points to a faith response that is not explicitly related to a particular historical revelation of God. . . . [It] provides a biblical basis for the possibility that the non-Israelite can also respond in saving faith to the creator, who is the God revealed in Israelite and Christian experience."[34] This "saving faith" is the sacred foundation of contemporary, secular memoir.

The Saving Faith of Contemporary Memoir

Some contemporary memoirists, as seen in the reflections of particular memoirs throughout this book, make references to specific religious traditions. Nancy Mairs reflects on her experience of becoming a Catholic; Richard Rodriguez is passionate in expressing the beneficial influence of the church in his life; and Heinz Kuehn tells of the spiritual wealth of Catholicism during his difficult teen years. Howard Kohn speaks glowingly of his father's involvement in the local Lutheran church. Brent Staples writes movingly about the faith of his mother, and Isabel Allende describes her encounter with a new Catholicism through the brave people who helped her and others survive the death threats of the military government in Chile.

Other contemporary memoirists cite experiences with explicit religious tradition that were negative, irrelevant, insufficient, or unhelpful in their search for life's meanings. Jill Ker Conway complains of the inability of the Judeo-Christian tradition to illuminate or interpret the geography of Australia. Tim McLaurin and his friends, on the eve of their induction into the marines, are advised by their town's minister to come forward and be saved. But he cannot bring himself to do so because he knows too well the lives of many of the people who populate the pews. Doris Grumbach leaves the Catholic church because of its treatment of women.

These authors' references to explicit religious tradition, whether positive or negative, do not, however, undergird these memoirs as their foundational orientation and expression. Instead, they rely on wisdom as the primal energy that motivates their memoirs. Wisdom is both a source of reflection and a mode of expression in these memoirs. Only on the surface does this suggest a loss of faith.

Nonfaith or Faith

John D. Barbour's book *Versions of Deconversion* subtitled, *Autobiography and the Loss of Faith,* examines how loss or change of faith shapes autobiographical writings. He identifies four characteristics of deconversion: (1) questioning or rejecting a belief system, (2) moral criticism, (3) emotional upheaval, and (4) rejection of community. He differentiates between deconversion and secularization by describing the latter as "a gradual fading away of beliefs, as religion simply ceases to inform a person's life, to make any real difference."[35] His claim that deconversion narratives mirror conversion narratives is intriguing and provocative. He further claims that religious studies and Christian theology need to pay careful attention to the insights of deconversion narratives as a way to self-definition. Barbour concludes that examining narratives that explore abandonment or change of faith could be vitally helpful in the work of interpreting faith to others.

Although I admire Barbour's work, I hesitate to identify the primary motif of many contemporary secular memoirs as deconversion. For many memoirists who have found the experience of a religious tradition valuable, religious tradition is but one of several sources of authority. Certainly for memoirists who have not found explicit religious tradition a helpful anchor and holy light for exploring, understanding, and interpreting their life, formal religious tradition does not function as a significant source of authority. Hence, Barbour's image of deconversion overemphasizes the exclusivity of an explicit religious tradition.

Doing Wisdom Theology

Explicit religious tradition is not a significant part of many contemporary, secular memoirs, but revelations of wisdom are still found there and can stir theological reflection. Such wisdom even apart from explicit religious tradition is by nature religious, and memoirs that rely on wisdom's revelation are surely theological reflection. Wisdom, as Roland Murphy points out, is a full and equal partner with explicit religious revelations like the Exodus experience and the Temple experience.

Wisdom is both the energizer and the capstone of contemporary, secular memoir. Wisdom, elusive and enigmatic graced reality, is recovered here and there in little bits and pieces in memoir. But even a remnant of wisdom, like a shard from a precious pot, reflects reality and illuminates its surroundings. Each memoir offers its own bit of wisdom, incomplete to be sure, but nonetheless impressive.

Wisdom is born of reflected experience and borne by imaginative expression of such introspection: in short, the memoir dynamic. Any wisdom, all wisdom, ultimately must be verified in the world of experience. "Knowledge is what you are taught, but Wisdom is what you bring to it," writes Canadian novelist Robertson Davies in *The Cunning Man*.[36]

Does the wisdom of any given memoir significantly illuminate real-world situations? If so, the memoir is a sacred text. Secular memoir, in its wisdom, is part of spiritual tradition while, at the same time, it stands sentinel at religion's gate to keep institutionalization at bay.

Conclusion

The reality of implicitly religious contemporary memoir invites reconsideration, reformulation, and, ultimately, reformation of certain definitions of and approaches to religion and spirituality. These memoirs, in addition to their transformational influence on religion and spirituality, safeguard religion and spirituality from turning inward, exclusively on themselves. They speak of the divine in the ordinary, of religion as real-world stuff, of sacramentality as a public event, and of spirituality as social and communal.

Without human experience, theology has no focus or purpose. Without stories of human experience, theologians have no foundation or data on which to operate. Without rumination upon stories of human experience, theological reflection has no relation or relevance to life and living.

The interplay of memory, reflection, imagination, and expression creates sacred texts. These sacred texts, stories of reflected-upon life events, embody and express individual and social, personal and communal significances. They reveal many things, but, most important, they reveal the transcendent dimensions of life. Things divine and the divine itself are made manifest through memoir. This does not happen through a grand synthesis of abstract theology or through an overwhelmingly charismatic hierophany, but in bits and pieces, in the shreds and shards of day-to-day experiences. ·

Like the Wisdom literature of the Bible, memoir provides real-world ballast to other forms and styles of theological inquiry and investigation. Through its descriptive narratives, memoir embraces an extraordinarily wide range of experiences and people. Through its emphasis on real-world experience, memoir becomes generative, supporting and inspiring future memoirists. In its totality as a sacred text, memoir contains and communicates wisdom.

"Ordinary Time": A Reflection

"Cafeteria Catholicism" has etched its way into the contemporary religious lexicon as a phrase that describes and denigrates people who disagree with some church teachings yet still remain members of the church. One bishop used this phrase so frequently in recent years that many people thought he had traded his miter for a chef's hat. The ingredient of informed conscience, too hard for this bishop to swallow, was clearly not in his larder.

Nancy Mairs' book *Ordinary Time* (Boston: Beacon Press, 1993) reflects both her loyalty to and her disagreements with Catholicism. Her faith most certainly would be labeled "Cafeteria Catholicism" by this marauding bishop masquerading as chef. Yet, the depth of her thinking coupled with the integrity of her conscience reveals both the bankruptcy and the abusiveness of the concept embodied in the phrase "Cafeteria Catholicism." *Ordinary Time* is a sacred story of wisdom emerging from experience. It is narrative theology to be sure.

Ordinary Time, that long span in the liturgical year from Pentecost to Advent, captures and communicates well this memoir's focal point. Though centered on the everyday, Mairs' reminiscences and reflections on her life are far from ordinary—much like many of the readings from the liturgical year cycle. She claims fierce allegiance both to Catholicism and to feminism, sometimes contradictory "isms." And among the events of ordinary time, her husband continues treatment for melanoma and she experiences the decline of independence brought on by advancing multiple sclerosis. She openly writes of her husband's infidelities and her own. These are but a few of the many and varied topics she explores.

The breadth of this book defies easy categorization, but the author herself helps to identify what she has created.

> I think of it as a kind of twentieth-century version of the spiritual autobiographies undertaken by my Puritan foremothers, which aims, as Mary G. Mason writes of Anne Bradstreet's brief "To My Dear Children," at a "harmonizing of the divine, the secular, and the personal, a unifying of a public and a private consciousness" by moving "from the inner circle of . . . husband, family, and community to the outward circle of God's providential creation." (7)

Ordinary time, the day in and day out quantities and qualities of life and living, manifests the miraculous for the author. "My motivation in writing *Ordinary Time* has been to examine this singular absolute of my existence: God is here. And here, and here, and here" (11). Mairs, by raising this wealth of revelation to consciousness again and again throughout her memoir, eschews a "one size fits all" Catholicism.

> The endless replication of a single system for structuring beliefs and behaviors in relation to the whole complicated world outside one's skin strikes me as a dangerous idea. We're all human, after all, and in deciphering life's ambiguities, each of us is bound to get at least one point wrong. Safer to recognize our fallibility, generate a number of different imaginative patterns, and share them freely. (8)

Some of her beliefs that diverge from this "single system for structuring beliefs and behaviors" center on birth control and abortion. Mairs explores her own experiences seriously, and these substantially, faithfully lead her to alternate orthodoxies. Yet at times she is winsome: "I think it would do someone like Cardinal Ratzinger a world of good to spend eighteen years rearing a child (though what it would do to the child worries me considerably)" (206).

Ordinary Time, the tale and trail of life and living, brings Nancy Mairs to Catholicism's door from her Congregational roots. Aesthetic gratification and social justice are, for her, the two intensely magnetic attractions of Catholicism. The former, a large part of her upbringing, reverberated in the Catholic tradition. "Today, each time I go through the Mass, I feel a frisson of recognition: I've been here before, I've been here for years and years" (71).

> I hadn't known many Catholics, not practicing ones anyway, and no religious at all. I'd heard plenty of tales about Catholic schools, of course, of being thwacked on the knuckles by fierce black-swaddled sisters with hairy warts on their chins, the tellers doomed somehow for the rest of their lives to recite their woes as compulsively as the Ancient Mariner, and with as little apparent relief. I didn't expect sisters in tennis shoes. I didn't expect sisters who spent their summer vacations with the farm workers, in the fields, in the camps, in the jails. I didn't expect sisters to run for the state legislature. And win. I didn't expect values to be preached so seldom and practiced so hard. If this was what went

on in a Catholic community, this commitment to action, at once light-hearted and dead-earnest . . . then what? (86)

The events of ordinary time—marriage, children, sickness—keep Mairs' "questions practical: What does it mean to live a life in God's presence? Present to God? What responsibilities do I bear in creating such a life? What choices must I make in order to sustain it?" (12). Her reflections on marriage as process, rather than marriage as pageant, call into serious question both the culture's and the church's attitude, rhetoric, and rite of marriage. Her reflections on children and motherhood, and on sickness, both her own fast-developing multiple sclerosis and her husband's melanoma, are real, to the point, and ultimately faith-filled. Although they are extraordinarily personal, her reflections also transcend the individual. They effectively embrace the social dimensions and implications of her specific experiences.

Ordinary time, marked today in America by the presence of homeless people, is yet another occasion for in-depth reflection. Mairs criticizes those who relegate the easing of social problems exclusively to the private sector; she excoriates George Bush's "thousand points of light" rhetoric as exceptionally parsimonious. "What speechwriter, I wonder, came up with an estimate so small in a country so vast, evoking brave scattered flickers of individual endeavor in the very heart of darkness?" (168). Generosity need not know such paltry boundaries.

"I don't want another church," Nancy Mairs tells her son-in-law, "I just want to get this one right" (99). An ambitious task, to be sure, for anyone, pope or peasant, but this author might well succeed. She had the advantage of being socialized into the church by a unique community.

The model I experienced . . . was one of inclusion rather than exclusion. Instead of being denied communion unless I converted, I was given communion until I felt strong enough to convert. The nourishing quality of the Eucharist, freely offered to anyone who's famished, has always been a central metaphor for me. I don't partake because I'm a good Catholic, holy and pious and sleek. I partake because I'm a bad Catholic, riddled by doubt and anxiety and anger: fainting from severe hypoglycemia of the soul. I need food. "O Holy One," I pray as I savor the host, "as this bread nourishes my body, so may your spirit nourish my soul. Grow strong within me, I pray, and let me live my life in your praise." God doesn't place conditions on the hungry. She feeds first and asks questions later. (89)

Might the bishop who so frequently served up the phrase "Cafeteria Catholicism" better have learned the chef's trade from Nancy Mairs? It might have done him, many other men, and some women a world of good to "pass over" this woman's experience; that is, to enter deeply into her memoir, "to walk a mile in her shoes," and then return to their own life with eyes that see anew. Ordinary Time, the concept, and *Ordinary Time*, the book, are far from ordinary.

"Parallel Time": A Reflection

Endless diatribes and discussions about race still reverberate within me, a product of a 1950s Chicago south side childhood. Many people who then lived on and around the twenty-five hundred block of West 110th Street, an area tucked just inside the city limits, had moved from "changing neighborhoods." A few of our neighbors had moved two and three times, at first underestimating how far and wide "they" would spread. "They're up to Sixty-seventh Street now." "They've jumped Halsted Street now." "They'll soon be past Seventy-ninth Street."

Not then identified as African American, "they" were formally called Negroes, informally referred to as "the Colored." Caustic names proliferated: niggers, jigs, and spooks. One Catholic pastor, like so many other people, used code language. From the pulpit he spoke of "the undesirables"; at late night Fathers' Club meetings, he, too, called them niggers and vowed to keep them out of his parish. Hardly moments or memories of glory for the Chicago Catholic church.

Brent Staples's memoir, *Parallel Time* (New York: Pantheon Books, 1994), whose title echoes Plutarch's classic work often known as *Parallel Lives*,[37] enfleshes the amorphous and anonymous "they" of my childhood in creatively disturbing and unusually haunting ways. Staples writes that he was on one side of the color line. I was on the other side of that color line. My life, like that of countless other whites, is parallel time to Brent Staples's life. Parallel lines, so geometricians say, never intersect, regardless of how far they extend. I would like to think that this geometric law need not be true of parallel times, and that my life and Staples's life really have met, at least in my reading of this memoir.

In telling his story, Staples created a sacred text for readers: the interplay of memory, reflection, imagination, and expression, a story of reflected-upon life events that embody and express individual and social, personal and communal significances. In bits and pieces, in the shreds and shards of his day-to-day experiences, Staples helps readers to reflect on their experience, to ponder their encounters with the sacred in their sisters and brothers, and to discover the wisdom in the encounters.

Before recalling his own childhood, the author begins his memoir by creating an icon of his brother: the events leading to his murder, the autopsy report, the trial. The strong, graphic words that capture his brother Blake, a drug dealer killed in a drug deal gone bad, are for Staples, like all icons, mysterious windows into God. This is another one of the many parallels of this memoir.

Staples's notions of time as "sneaky and elastic" were forever fixed by his childhood.

> This fixation had come from the way my family lived. We moved all the time. We went on and on like bedouins with couches, tables, and mattresses jumbled in the backs of pickup trucks. We moved as the family grew. We moved when my parents were separated and again when they reconciled. We moved when we fell behind in the rent. We moved when the sheriffs put our furniture on the sidewalk. We moved after the family had pounded a house to pieces. We'd had seven different addresses by the time I reached the eighth grade. That's why I was never where I was. The move was out there lurking, just off the mental shore. Best to be ready when it came. . . .
>
> The chaos of these nights exhausted even the deepest goodwill. The friends and relatives who helped us drove up in their trucks to find us dashing through the house, hurling things into boxes. First they grumbled under their breaths. Then they withdrew into sullen reveries. We raced to move the heavy things before these helpers quit. This meant triage with the furniture, abandoning bedsteads and couches where they stood. If the new house was close enough, we carried the small things by hand. We became a caravan of children, with lamps and end tables in hand, strung out like bedouins down the street. (11–12)

In addition to a houseful of brothers and sisters, Staples's growing-up years were crammed full of neighborhood characters and extended family, among them Mr. and Mrs. Prince, neighborhood grocery store owners who drove impressively huge Cadillacs—Mr. Prince's car had "the gas cap ingeniously hidden in the taillight" (26); many indomitable women who kept their eyes on the street activity and freely disciplined troublemaking children; Gene, a gay beautician who animated the women's lives both with wit and wisdom; Bunny, Staples's uncle who "changed cars as often as he did shirts" (32); Mattie Walker, the girl next door; and Triboletti, the pharmacist who practiced medicine. Staples recalls his brother Blake, who had chronic ear infections, being treated by the pharmacist rather than the doctor:

"Triboletti understood our situation; it was the same as everyone else's. We had a sick child; we had money for either medicine or diagnosis but not both" (98).

Unique neighborhood places abound: sandwich shops standing next to slaughterhouses "where pigs screamed all the time" (31); and Andy's Musical Bar, in whose shadow the Staples family lived for a time.

One of the family's myriad moves, this time to the Polish West End, brings Brent into contact with a white, ethnic, Catholic world.

> The Polish and Ukrainian boys were alluringly exotic. They had unpronounceable names and ate unpronounceable foods. They were Catholics, a new species to me. They smudged their foreheads with ash and ate fish on Friday. They told a priest their sins at confession and counted their prayers on beaded necklaces. I longed to see their houses and know their secrets. The Polish and Ukrainian boys didn't see it that way. They tolerated me, but in a way that made me invisible. When I think of the Polish West End, I think of a closed circle of backs, the reddened backs of necks and the greasy slopes of pompadours. (62)

Staples was cursed at in Ukrainian and Polish as he walked the area. Polish boys yelled, "Way ta go Stash" (58) to all their teammates during their baseball games as if they all had this same name. A neighborhood Catholic school, Saint Hedwig's, incarnated the Catholic stereotype: nuns in black, errant boys "snatched into line with neck-breaking force" (68), and the talk of burning in hell for all eternity.

Uniformed girls from another neighborhood Catholic school, Resurrection, sing out a parody as they passed Brent on the street.

> They were singing "The Duke of Earl," which was just out that fall. I was well past them before I realized that they were singing "Spook" instead of "Duke": "Spook, spook, spook, of earl, spook, spook, spook of earl," in descending chords, to the tune of the song. . . . The Catholics were all the same: spiteful and mean. (72)

The combination of Catholic understanding of sin, penalties for sins, and confession was a conundrum to Brent.

> My mother's theology was easier to live with. Her view was that Christian spirit resided not in words or ritual but in everyday

conduct. God was in people, she said, not in buildings. You didn't need preachers to live a Christian life; that you could do on your own. Hence we could miss church for years on end without penalty. If you lived a Christian life you could expect a Christian welcome when you died. If you didn't, you couldn't. Feed the hungry, clothe the naked, keep free of malice, and you had it made. I was uncertain of what malice was, but sure that I could keep clear of it. (69)

Staples's mother did live her beliefs by inviting down-and-out people to share their home: two pregnant women who came to term on the family's living room sofa, a gigolo, the one-handed Mr. Tommy, and an aging softball player. All of these were among the recipients of Mrs. Staples's particular practice of Christianity.

Brent Staples's psyche enlarged after they moved once again, this time into the shadow of Community Methodist church. He became part of a theater group at the church, and he participated in another play at the Friends Chester House Project, a Quaker community organization. He attended a Quaker retreat, became involved in the Swarthmore College Afro-American society. After graduating from high school, he met, through the League of Women Voters, Eugene Sparrow who enticed him into Project Prepare, an intensive educational program for "at-risk" people. Gone forever were his thoughtless childhood activities of petty theft, easy sex, and halfhearted attempts at street fighting.

After successful completion of his undergraduate studies, Staples received a Ford Foundation grant. He went to the University of Chicago where people extended a warm, though at times, condescending welcome to him. He rented a wonderfully spacious old Chicago apartment quite unlike the cramped quarters of his years at home. Although he loved to walk the University of Chicago neighborhood known as Hyde Park, he quickly became aware of just how wary most white people were of any black male on a darkened side street late at night. At times he aired his frustrations by taunting white people on the streets after nightfall. Hyde Park became his refuge and his strength.

Although he studied psychology, he was perhaps even better educated by novelist Saul Bellow. *Dangling Man*,[38] Bellow's first novel narrated in journal form, and *Humboldt's Gift*,[39] a later novel, motivated Staples to carry his own journal everywhere and fill it. At times his fascination with this novelist's work was so great that his behavior bordered on stalking fellow neighborhood resident Saul Bellow. More than Staples's psychology studies, Bellow's novels prepared Staples for his life's work. Even though he finished his Ph.D. in psychology, and taught part-time at his undergraduate college, full-time faculty positions were scarce. He turned to writing where he has been ever since, fortunately.

Brent Staples concludes his memoir where he began, with his brother's death. He realizes that, unlike what so many white people want to hear, it was *chance* that separated him from the ghetto and from his brother's fate.

> Chance wasn't popular as explanation. People preferred a story about an individual who triumphs over all through force of character. The least charitable of these people cited me as proof that the American dream was alive and well—if only those shiftless bastards in the slums would reach for it. Once I'd kept a wry distance on this process and accepted the halo when it was given. Blake's murder changed this. Now I could see that my "escape" from the ghetto was being marshaled as evidence against him. This role I no longer wished to play. (260)

This memoir, more than reminiscent of Plutarch's famous title, recollects the purpose of *Parallel Lives*. Plutarch wanted to encourage mutual respect between two different peoples, the Greeks and the Romans of his day. Staples's memoir, a contemporary equivalent, subtitled *Growing Up in Black and White,* might also engender more respect among different peoples of our day. *Parallel Time* could be helpful reading to understand what happens on the south side of Chicago, and on all the south sides that exist in the world.

Reflective Exercises

❖ Go through the lectionary, the official readings for both weekday and Sunday worship. See how many of them are taken from the Wisdom literature of the Hebrew Scriptures.

❖ In addition to feminism, what examples of "the world evangelizing the church" can you think of?

❖ What comes to mind when you hear the word *theology?* Recall some examples of narrative theology in your own life.

❖ What does the word *sacrament* mean to you? Does describing a memoir as a sacrament expand your ideas of sacrament? What does it do for your understanding of memoir?

❖ Do you agree with James Hopewell that "the authority of Scripture, dogma, organization, and theological reasoning that once constituted the church . . . has waned to the point of inconsequentiality for most Christians trying to make sense of their existence"? Do you think that memoir can speak with religious authority?

❖ Mairs says that "God is here." Recall your most vivid memory of God being here.

❖ Graph your religion story: those highs and lows of your experience with religion. Reflect on one high point and then do the same with a low point.

❖ When you were growing up, what was your neighborhood like? Whom do you remember? What incidents capture the essence of living there? What do these tell you about yourself and about your family?

❖ What is your single most important life experience from your life that shaped your attitude toward race or ethnicity?

❖ What do you remember about your "mother's [or father's] theology"? Was it easy or hard to live with?

4

The Memoir Dynamic

Introduction

The forms of memoir are many, with numerous styles within each form. Some memoirs remember and express the significance of certain life events of a specific individual. Other memoirs, social and communal in nature, remember and express the significance of the experiences of an entire people. Nonetheless, even the most individual and personal memoir reflects worlds larger than one person. Likewise, the most social and communal memoir reflects a single style and tone. Many memoirs are developed outside of specific religious traditions. In other memoirs, specific religious traditions play a major role. All authentic memoirs, however, regardless of origin, are icons of experience, which makes them sacred texts.

One consistent dynamic undergirds the varied forms and styles of memoir: recollection of a given experience, reflection on that experience, and communication of the reflected experience. Memory recalls experience. Concentration, focus, perspective, comparison, and contrast fuel the reflection. Communication of reflected experience relies on verbal skills—either oral or written—a sense of audience, and a willingness to share personally significant events and their meanings. This energy culminates in an artistic form—an icon—that embodies and expresses experience and reflection on experience. While this memoir dynamic appears orderly in theory, it is never so tidy in actual practice. The four stages of the memoir dynamic—recollection, reflection, communication, and iconography—overlap, intertwine, intermingle, and illuminate. This chapter describes an anatomy of this memoir dynamic.

The Memoir Mileposts

Memoir is marked by two mileposts. The first milepost is the moment of the event or experience itself, and the second milepost is the moment when a memoir takes form, be it hours, days, months, or years later.

Borrowing a phrase from Kathleen Norris's memoir, *Dakota: A Spiritual Geography,* I name the area between these two mileposts spiritual geography.[1] The word *spiritual* indicates the unseen, real dimensions of life and living that make us uniquely human and also indicates that God is near in all of life. Geography is the study of the earth and its life. Land, air, and sea, plant and animal life, people and their industries, all are objects of study for the geographer. Spiritual geography charts the intangible qualities of life and living, feelings and emotions, motivations and meanings, beliefs and values that are life giving.

Marking Milepost One

How one chooses events from one's past—the first memoir milepost—to recall, reflect on, and relate is sometimes spontaneous, sometimes very deliberate. The answer one gives to the oft asked question "How was your day?" depends on the depth and sincerity of the question, who is posing it, how much energy one has at the end of the day to respond, and how much time is available for the answer. The subjects of more studied memoirs might well be determined by other factors.

Some memoirs focus on unusual, traumatic, or unique experiences. For example, many memoirs have been written by prisoners of war, such as those by persons held hostage during the U.S. Embassy takeover in Iran. Other memoirs focus on connections with current events or history. After his fall from power and grace, Mikhail Gorbachev penned a memoir entitled *The August Coup*.[2] Still other memoirs zero in on untold or seldom-told stories. Sally Morgan's memoir, *My Place,* for example, reflects upon her family's practice of hiding that they were Aboriginal Australians.[3] Yet other memoirs celebrate ordinary, day-to-day experiences. Ken Carey's 1994 memoir, *Flat Rock Journal,* as the subtitle indicates, is about a day in the Ozark Mountains.[4]

Memoir's first milepost need not be fettered to single events or to contiguous time periods. Some memoirs follow a theme, focusing on a series of related incidents or events. In such memoirs, what I have identified as the first milepost is actually a motif running throughout a person's experience. These related, recurring experiences become one, unified by a common theme. Richard Rodriguez's 1992 memoir, *Days of Obligation,* for instance, describes and ponders experiences linked by his understanding of national identity in a multicultural world.[5]

Between the Mileposts

Between the event that triggers the movement toward memoir and the moment of memoir, surveying the spiritual geography is crucial to the memoir dynamic. Ideally this period fosters reflection, soul-searching, and more developed understandings of the original event. Good memory can aid the process of memoir, but the ability to take time to reflect seriously upon experience is essential.

A person rushing to publish a memoir of a recent event might well capture her or his fifteen minutes of fame and haul in a load of money. Such scam memoirs, hastily penned to turn a profit from the momentary limelight, contain little if any serious and substantial reflection that, to use Robertson Davies' vocabulary, reveals a subtext of one's life events.[6] In short, exploration of the spiritual geography is missing.

The instantaneous quality of contemporary communication militates against plumbing the depths and taking the measure of the spiritual geography of life's experiences and events: "The public gets more and more submissive to instant history."[7] Roman Catholic Bishop Kenneth Untener once remarked, "Instant news is doing to reflective thinking what fast-food is doing to dining."

Telecommunications both foster and feed an appetite for immediacy. What is happening right now or better yet what is about to happen captures attention. The "news" takes priority over serious analysis and reflection on what has already happened. This ever-present nowness, the ever-growing quantity of information available through cable and satellite television and the Internet, leaves little room for reflection on and learning from past events. This feeding frenzy for immediacy offers an unbalanced diet. Reflection becomes an endangered species in such an ecosystem.

Consequently, time and space for reflection is certainly undervalued and at times nonexistent in popular culture. The one-minute manager becomes the thirty-second manager. And a contemporary proverb of people within corporations that are attempting serious and substantial downsizing, "If you are employed, you are doing the work of two people," suggests how rare any sort of reflective time has become in the business world. Serious, substantial, and sustained reflection is considered frivolous by shortsighted, productivity-oriented personnel. Reflection becomes countercultural.

Precincts that foster such reflection are also rare. Some religious traditions foster reflection by providing physical and psychic space for reflection. Retreat centers supply physical space for people who wish to think deeply about their life, without disturbance. Certain religious rituals and rites are occasions for reflection: for example, the Jewish Day of Atonement (Yom Kippur) and the Catholic sacrament of reconciliation, popularly known as confession. Such places and rituals of religious traditions concretely embody theological theories. In this respect, many religious traditions oppose in practice some current trends by offering these alternative experiences to their members and in some instances extend these practices to people outside their own membership.

Like every other human endeavor, not all religious traditions provide such freedom within their physical and psychic spaces. The controlling environments generated by some religious sects coupled with fundamentalist approaches to religious writings and doctrines militate against people using their religious traditions for genuine exploration of and reflection on life experiences. Such situations and approaches, like scam memoirs, are ultimately sacrilegious because they misuse the sacred trust that religion ideally elicits from its officials and its activities. They denigrate the sacred stories of ordinary people.

The therapeutic process is another precinct for reflection. Psychiatrists and psychologists offer formal opportunities for in-depth reflection and analysis of one's life. The work of James W. Fowler, especially his adult development theory, provides yet another helpful vantage point for reflection.[8] Less formal therapeutic processes take the form of twelve-step programs modeled after the successful approach of Alcoholics Anonymous.

Sabbaticals and research leaves, longtime hallmarks of higher education and recently emulated by a handful of innovative corporations, serve the reflective needs of a fortunate few. The term *sabbatical* has biblical roots. Every seventh year the fields of the Israelites were to remain fallow in order to renew and regenerate the land.

Serious conversation with a friend, a solitary walk, a getaway in the country or by the shore, or a quiet room at home all offer other opportunities for reflection in the midst of a culture increasingly hostile to such activity.

Memory and perspective on memory through reflection—surveying the spiritual geography—form the foundation of memoir. The quality of each memoir is linked essentially to the quality of reflection that follows the life event and precedes the articulation of that event. The interpretation of the event that eventually gets embodied, either implicitly or explicitly, in memoir is gestated and given birth by reflection. Allowing time and finding space for reflection to flourish are necessarily intrinsic parts of the memoir dynamic.

Marking Milepost Two

Having reflected upon important experiences, a person arrives at the second milepost on the journey to memoir: the moment when one consciously chooses to develop a specific icon of a given experience. In effect this second milepost reaches back to the original experience or event and brings it into this present moment. The proverb "Your view depends upon your point of view" captures the importance of this second milepost.

Like the first milepost, this "moment" is usually a much longer period of time, and the moment one elects to establish as this second milepost is voluntary and subjective. A person might wait for days, weeks, months, or years before starting to shape memoir. The time taken before the second milepost influences the nature of the memoir; therefore, milepost two adds another indisputable element of subjectivity to memoir.

This particular moment of memoir, the time a person decides to relate event and reflection on that event, is a strong determinant of the final product. For example, Mikhail Gorbachev's memoir, *The August Coup,* would have differed markedly had he penned it before his fall from power and grace rather than afterward. Change the position of the second milepost, and one alters the memoir dynamic and the memoir icon. The period of reflection, the spiritual geography, either expands or contracts by the placement of the second milepost. The specific perspective of one given moment is replaced by the perspective of another given moment, hence altering the memoir slightly or substantially.

In his book *World of Wonders,* Canadian novelist Robertson Davies writes about a "confessional moment"; that time in a person's life when one decides to reveal the subtext, "a reality running like a subterranean river under the surface; an enriching, but not necessarily edifying, background to what is seen."[9] The confessional moment is the point in life when people are willing and able to reveal their subtext.

Davies' idea of the confessional moment is intriguing, but limited by the traditional definitions and understandings of autobiography. By contextualizing Davies' valuable insight of confessional moment within the memoir dynamic, the confessional moment becomes many confessional moments. Every person has many throughout life. Some are more significant than others. They are all possible occasions for establishing this second milepost of the memoir dynamic.

Words: More Than Currency

After the recollection, reflection, and the confessional moment have arrived, the memoirist is called to compose the words of memoir. Initially these words might well only be utterances, random doodles, or jottings, none having much precision nor communicative quality.

Words, recognizable and communicative, are at the heart of memoir. The vocabulary a person uses gives one's experience a recognizable and specific form. The English language, American poet Walt Whitman writes, "is brawny enough and limber and full enough"[10] to more than adequately communicate the text and subtext of a person's or a group's life experience to others.

Words seldom, if ever, quit. Emily Dickinson writes in a poem numbered 1212:

> A word is dead
> When it is said,
> Some say.
> I say it just
> Begins to live
> That day.[11]

Dickinson knew that in addition to communicating facts, words also shape perspective, one's view on a point of view, and establish meaning, the why of incidents and events. Language functions not only as a means for conveying our ideas to others, but also as an agency that shapes what we see: "Our way of dividing the world and classifying its components is significantly influenced by the linguistic system that we have learned to use."[12]

Meanings of events and experiences are established in large part through choice of language. The denotations and connotations of words within the same language vary from household to household, from region to region, from country to country. *John* in one household might mean the bathroom, while in another household it might be the first name of a family member. The words *neutral ground* in New Orleans refer to parkways in the middle of roads. In other regions of the United States this phrase, whatever it may convey, certainly has nothing to do with its meaning in New Orleans. In many places that were part of the former British Commonwealth, the word *diary* refers to an appointment book, while in the United States it means a personal journal.

Memoir is embodied in words—oral or written. And even with the difficulties in communicating precise meanings, words do participate in the construction of meaning. People who listen attentively and read carefully develop abilities to sense meaning manifested by choice of words. Counselors and therapists, for example, are trained to listen carefully to the words of their clients to gain access into their meaning structure, into their present problem, and, ultimately, into their real difficulties. So even when the hard work of reflection has come to a ripeness in a confessional moment, the fruit forms in the mysterious shaping of words.

The Iconography of Memoir

The process of the memoir dynamic leads to a product, a work of art: memoir. While words are its medium, every artistically cast memoir takes on a life of its own. People encounter memoir, form a relationship with it, or reject it. Its artistry exercises a major influence on such decisions, but the many and various impressions, attitudes, and feelings people bring to any work of art, memoir included, are extraordinarily subjective. It is in this relationship with memoir's artistic expression that merit and meaning ultimately reside. The meaning of any given memoir can thus vary from person to person, contributing further to memoir's postmodern, subjective quality.

Memoirs can be either oral or written. If a memoir is oral, it must somehow be captured in order to preserve its iconography. Sound recording devices, either by themselves or in conjunction with videotapes, capture oral memoir. Ross Talarico has developed another method for creating icons of oral memoirs. He listens to people who are unable to read or write as they tell stories from their lives. Then he writes poems that capture their stories, their mood, and the significance of their stories. He has published these poems in a book titled *Hearts and Times: The Literature of Memory*.[13] This process preserves life experiences that otherwise probably would be lost forever. This process of capturing oral memoir dramatically points out the importance of iconography in memoir.

Beyond the Mileposts

This memoir dynamic continues in the experiences of those who encounter the product, oral or written. The dynamic has the capacity to influence people beyond the author's own friendship circle and beyond the author's own life span.

Encounter with memoir is an occasion to enter another life empathically. Another person's memoir can help people, as stated in a Native American prayer, "walk a mile in our neighbor's moccasins." It allows people to experience a version of reality from the inside. It is perhaps one of the oldest forms of what people today think of as virtual reality, the ability to accurately simulate an experience through technology. Memoir takes a person out of one's own world, and immerses one in the world of another person.

The dynamic continues when the readers of a memoir then consider their own life. The experience of encountering another's memoir becomes a new lens through which to view one's own life events. Theologian John Dunne terms this process of immersing oneself in another person's life and then returning to one's own life as "passing over." Jon Nilson, once a student of Dunne's and now a scholar of his thought, summarizes this process clearly:

> Passing over means entering into the standpoint of another person, age, or culture and thereby gaining new understanding. Passing over means temporarily adopting another and different perspective on common concerns and thus discovering truths about oneself, others, and God which could not have been found solely within the confines of one's own standpoint. It is followed by "coming back" or returning to the standpoint of one's own life and times. Yet this standpoint is now different, because it has

been expanded and enriched by the truths discovered in passing over.[14]

One person's memoir occasionally becomes someone else's milepost. Reading someone's memoir becomes an experience worthy of the reader's reflections. The reader then gains perspective through the immersion with the experience of the memoir. In some cases, the original memoir moves a person, after serious and substantial reflection, to some action. Eventually that person might create a reflection on action motivated by the original memoir, a memoir on memoir so to speak.

Dayton Duncan's book *Out West* is such an example.[15] After reading Lewis and Clark's journals, studying them carefully, and reflecting on their significance, he set out to recreate the journey's route using modern modes of transportation rather than canoes and trailblazing. His memoir of the experience reflects well on life today in comparison to and contrast with Lewis and Clark's day.

Back to the Future

There is yet another dimension to the memoir dynamic: the future. On the surface it sounds strangely anachronistic and oxymoronic because memoir is so often associated exclusively with the past. But visions of the future, be they utopian or apocalyptic, contribute to interpretation of one's life events, which in turn influence meaning and guide the craft of memoir creation.

The future also functions as an intended, determining audience for recorded memoir. Motivated by generativity, it is common for each person, at various points in life, to want to contribute something to the pool of wisdom for those who will follow. One's own children, grandchildren, great-grandchildren are immediate and striking reminders that it is well worth the time and energy to preserve and pass on wisdom. Children provide a significant motivation for many people to write their own memoirs.

Some preliterate cultures, as was mentioned in chapter 2, developed a custom of elderly members telling their tribe's stories to certain younger members. This tradition accomplished two objectives. First, it provided a structure to ensure transmission of wisdom from one generation to succeeding generations. Second, because there were in some groups taboos against telling stories of one's life to people outside the tribe, it kept the tribe's developed wisdom exclusively within its own group. Black Elk, the Oglala Sioux medicine man who told his life stories to John Neihardt, has been criticized by some tribal members for giving away part of their tribe's wisdom to outsiders. Black Elk apparently had a broader interpretation of who was eligible to receive his collected wisdom. And, since the 1960s, vast numbers of outsiders have appreciated the opportunity Black Elk extended to wider worlds as evidenced by his book's perennial popularity.

In U.S. culture today, when compared to prior ages, nothing is too personal for mass consumption. The current popularity of talk shows fosters a search for some of the strangest topics being aired, and facilitates a tell-all syndrome. These shows are the telecommunication equivalent to written scam memoirs.

Conclusion

Like a carefully wound spring in a Swiss mantle clock or a tiny battery in a digital wristwatch, the memoir dynamic energizes life stories. Unlike the precision of these timepieces, however, the memoir dynamic moves less certainly, starts and stops without conscious cause, and produces various unlike results.

Although there is little if any uniformity among them, there is a unity to memoirs, namely the process by which they are initially formulated and finally expressed. That process, the memoir dynamic, is a defining characteristic of what it means to be human. Participation in that process is a recognition of what one life means for the rest of humanity. It is also a call to generosity and generativity.

"Mixed Blessings": A Reflection

Even after a person has choked down shelves of quick-fix, self-help books, even after a person has dipped into spiritual resources from fundamentalist to New Age, the care and tending of one's inner world remains a lifelong, challenging, demanding project.

In contemporary Christianity, models of spirituality and methods of growing in the spiritual life are as wide and varied as this big-tent religion itself. One precinct favors spiritual direction; other precincts favor small-group experiences, from psychologically-oriented twelve-step programs to scripturally-oriented Base Communities; yet another precinct, formally organized into prelatures, reputes to favor a medieval amalgam of unswerving obedience and self-flagellation conducted in clandestine groups. Many Catholic parents who send their kids to parochial school or parish religious education classes hope against sometimes formidable odds that their offspring will be introduced to worthwhile spiritualities.

Heinz R. Kuehn's memoir, *Mixed Blessings* (Athens, GA: University of Georgia Press, 1988), will not be found in a bookstore's self-help section, nor will it propound a model of spirituality currently in vogue underneath the big tent. Yet the ways in which the author attends to his inner world as he matures during an unseemly epoch of history are impressive and substantial. His memoir also shows how events long past but reflected on over time mature into profound reflections on contemporary life.

"I had been fourteen when Hitler had come to power, twenty when the war began. I was now twenty-six and had come out of six years of war alive and unscathed" (169). This memoir's subtitle, *An Almost Ordinary Life in Hitler's Germany,* sounds ironically understated from today's vantage point. Newsreels of bulldozers pushing the corpses of innumerable concentration camp victims into mass graves, of survivors' skeletal torsos teetering on their matchstick legs, icons of horror, look extraordinary.

Kuehn's personal life was also far from ordinary. The frequently powerful chemistry of Catholic and Jewish intermarriages (well documented by J. D. Salinger's Glass family stories)[16] is present even though Kuehn's parents divorced when Heinz was just six. His mother's family, particularly the grandparents, give Heinz a feel for the extraordinary in the ordinary.

As Orthodox Jews, Markus and his family may have resented
Mother's indifference to her religion, but they treated Annemarie
[Heinz's sister] and me as if we had been their own children.
They included us in the routine of a life where nothing seemed
ultimately important but where everything appeared in some in-
definable way joyfully solemn. The freedom we were permitted
in their house, their town, was not the kind of moody, lonely
freedom that weighed on us in Berlin. Here, the day's tasks and
affairs were set into a frame of rituals and habits that brought
moods and thoughts home, from wherever they had strayed, to a
shelter of serenity, and a mystery I could not name gave a tone
of freshness and a ring of happiness to even the most ordinary
household chores. Here, it was not the Paradise above a soaring
Gothic portal but the *mezuzah* (among Orthodox Jews, a piece
of parchment with biblical inscriptions, rolled up in a small con-
tainer, and attached to the doorpost as the biblical passages command) on the doorframe of Markus's house that closed off a
sacred space from the intrusions of the marketplace. Here it was
not the chanting of the canons but the voice of Markus, his rap-
id, plaintive singsong that, awakening Annemarie and me, gave
an air of festivity to the breaking day. Here, sitting at a table covered with embroidered linen and set with things of silver and
precious-looking china, breaking the brittle disks of matzo by the
light of candles, I was not a spectator but a participant drawn
into an inexplicable and deeply exciting ritual. I was too young
to understand what I saw and felt, but I sensed that these
prayers, these rituals, this table, this meal were the source of the
lightheartedness, the smiling openness, the spirited gaiety that
drew me to this couple. I knew homesickness—I would know it
throughout my childhood—but in Gilgenburg I had no thought,
no longing for Father or Mother, or for Berlin, the city where I
belonged. (27–28)

His father's influence, more elusive during Heinz's early years,
blossoms as he matures. Study and scholarship, philosophy and theology, behavior and ethics are serious and substantial center points of
his father's inner world and, eventually, of his own. After several failed
marriages, his father, a thinker and writer, finds peace and content-
ment during the final years of the war living on the grounds of a
Benedictine convent outside Berlin. Kuehn reflects on his father, "I
believe he was temperamentally destined for a life of solitude, and no

marriage, no matter how successfully lived, would have touched the core of his being" (10). Kuehn frequently visits his father at this Benedictine convent and eventually lives there during the final years of the war. At the outset of the war, while working in the State Labor Service and wearing the national uniform, Heinz visits his father. The confrontation between father and son reveals the strong personalities and positions of each man.

> "Take that rag off," he hissed, pointing at the armband emblazoned with the swastika. "Take off the whole Goddamned outfit if you want me to talk to you." His outburst was not unexpected. I closed the door behind me, sat down on the sofa, and, while he kept his back turned to me, staring out of the window, talked. "Look," I began, "I will walk out of here if you wish, but that will be the last time you will see me. I know you love me; that I love you, and respect you, goes without saying. You think you know me and understand me. That's true—when it comes to books, religion, ideas, opinions. But what do you know about my life? You sit here in your room, reading and writing and when you meet people they are of your kind, of your persuasion. You sit here, peacefully waiting out the end of Nazi Germany. You don't have to mingle with people of all kinds about whose views on Hitler or whatever you don't know anything. I do, every day. I have to mingle with them and deal with them. Your identity card shows 'Richard Kühn.' Period. Mine shows 'Heinz Richard Kühn. Mischling Ersten Grades' [mixed breed of the first degree]. Your identity is unsullied. Mine is branded, stamped, marked. Oh yes, I agree with you that Hitler and his ilk are despicable, hateful, evil personified. But you don't have to wear the man's uniform and insignia. I do, and if I refuse I will be shot." (70)

Kuehn eschews the martyr's role. Nor does he flee Germany as do his mother and his other Jewish relatives. Instead he stays, living day by day, working at jobs considered useful by the Reich, moving from one place to another when his quarters get bombed. As a young, healthy-looking male not in military service, he is assumed to be Jewish, half-true and half-false.

Amid the chaos, the violence, and the continual uncertainty of these years, Heinz assiduously attends to his inner world. Books and small groups of intellectually curious people with whom he discusses ideas are his two principal means of developing his spirituality.

"Books were my link to Father. They were his substitute in the apartment and a never-ending topic of our conversations when we visited, and the strongest means he had to exert his influence on my development" (22). As Kuehn grew, books continued to form and reform his inner world.

The other strong influence on his inner world, small groups of intellectually curious people, is best exemplified in an intimate, ongoing gathering known as the Thomas Circle under the direction of Hermann Joseph Schmidt, the student chaplain of the Berlin diocese, nicknamed Hejo by the students in the group.

> Hejo kept testing and measuring, patiently taking us step by step from what we saw, heard, and felt to the ultimate source, meaning, and purpose of existence. "Mr. Raubusch," he would say, addressing a young man in the black officers' uniform of the Panzer divisions, "in training your men, have you ever used the word 'courage'? Obviously you have. Now has it ever occurred to you that there might be an essential link between courage and humility? That one cannot truly exist without the other? It hasn't. Well, let's see what Saint Thomas has to say about the connection in the *Secunda secundae*" (the second part of the second book of the *Summa theologiae*). He tried to meet us where we lived, and after taking us to the dizzying heights of a universe where everything, from the pebble on the beach to the glory of the Trinity, hangs together, he would lead us back to our own closed-in microcosm that suddenly seemed too tight, too dark, too empty. "Miss Heller," he might challenge one of the women, "you once said that Baudelaire is the most significant Christian poet of the nineteenth century. We have spent the last few evenings discussing Saint Thomas's views on 'tristitia'—sadness. For him, despondent sadness is the root of vindictiveness, or hatred and anger. Now, did his, if you will, metaphysical dissection of gloom in any way help you to understand something about *Les fleurs du mal* that eluded you?" (104)

Kuehn's inner world, fed both by the classics and by contemporary books, and digested with small groups of people, sometimes just father and son, other times fellow students with their teacher, still other times at the Benedictine priory with people of his father's generation, grows alongside the cataclysmic events of the outer world.

Published after more than forty years between the event and the telling of the event, Heinz Kuehn's memoir of his coming of age looks oddly out of date on the surface. Many people have long since given up on the concept or relevance of unified systems of knowledge, replacing them with more eclectic, personalized constructs of reality. Few people today consistently read books of substance. Nor do they participate in sustained conversation with small groups of people who search for in-depth understandings. Such activities have largely been replaced by passive television and video viewing.

Yet this memoir offers more than déjà vu for people of the author's generation, and more than a nostalgic wandering into a past age for subsequent generations. *Mixed Blessings* stands as testimony to the lifelong, challenging, demanding nature of tending to one's inner world and spiritual geography. This memoir also functions as a critique of some contemporary spiritualities.

The philosophical and theological systems of Kuehn's inner world were not blindly swallowed by his contemporaries, but acted as frameworks for exploration and integration. They encouraged thought and engendered investigation of ultimate questions, an activity so necessary in contemporary religious education. Critical reading of a wide variety of texts, both classic and contemporary, provided a substantial knowledge base for study and discussion among Kuehn, his friends, and associates, and it is sorely needed in some middle-class Christian Base Communities. And ideas, so apparent in Heinz Kuehn's world, need to be incorporated into substantive spiritual direction for any educated person.

"To Teach": A Reflection

Too poor for a tutor, kerosene, pen, or paper, so the story goes, young Abraham Lincoln schooled himself by light of the hearth fire, writing lessons on the face of a shovel with charcoal bits. The idyllic image of Lincoln's log cabin education, soothing as a sweet dream, stands in stark contrast to the nightmares today's schools precipitate. When Jonathan Kozol wrote *Death at an Early Age* in 1967, the title referred to the destruction of young students' hearts and minds.[17] Today, metal detectors at schoolhouse doors give witness to public education as another killing field in urban America. Death in schools is sometimes no longer metaphoric.

Grand rhetoric and grandiose plans attempt to quell our fright about schools. George Bush wanted to be known as the education president. As he strutted full stage in the international theater, his domestic cameo appearances did little if anything to establish such a reputation. The voucher plan that he touted, which would channel public money into private schools via parental choice, was soundly defeated in November 1992 in a California referendum. And Christopher Whittle, founder of the channel 1 news program for schools, momentarily captured headlines in 1992 when he wooed Benno Schmidt away from the presidency of Yale to develop a private, for-profit school system known as the Edison Project. Summer 1995 witnessed the mayor of New York City exhorting the public school system there to model itself after Catholic schools.

Catholic schools, too, cause sleepless nights, though for radically different reasons. Closed and consolidated Catholic schools continue to contribute to their church's ongoing identity crisis. For many, American Catholicism was and, for some, still is "the church that was a school."[18] Today, as more and more dioceses slip precariously close to bankruptcy, there is less and less money to fund remaining Catholic schools. Yet, today's Catholic schools receive high marks from a variety of public sources. They are no longer dismissed as elitist institutions summarily expelling troublesome students to public schools. Their student bodies reflect the many diversities of contemporary America. Catholic schools are heralded as educational communities that could well serve as models to right what is so desperately wrong in many precincts of public education.

William Ayers awakens us momentarily from our national educational nightmare in *To Teach: The Journey of a Teacher* (New York: Teachers College, Columbia University, 1993). His credentials are put forth by Herbert Kohl who wrote in the foreword:

> Bill Ayers speaks as teacher, parent, and student: as compassionate observer and passionate advocate of his three sons and of all our children. What is unique about this book is the way in which the personal and professional merge seamlessly. Ayers does not separate his family life from his work, or fall into a professional mode when he deals with other people's children." (ix)

Like many great memoirs, *To Teach* arose out of Ayers' need to articulate a vision, specifically his need to formulate an antidote to the desperation so many people feel over the state of education. His years of experience as a student, teacher, and parent are the wellspring of his wisdom. Like many memoirists, he does not follow a careful chronology, but employs story to explain and instruct.

Ayers believes that teaching is a "powerful calling" seldom nurtured in the professional preparation of teachers and almost never nourished by policies and procedures present in many schools and school systems. By tapping into this powerful calling rather than mastering spiritually bankrupt managerial myths about teaching (he lists and discusses ten of them), teachers themselves will be the agents that reform and renew schools.

> Good teaching requires most of all a thoughtful, caring teacher committed to the lives of students. So simple and, in turn, somehow so elegant. Like mothering or parenting, good teaching is not a matter of specific techniques or styles, plans or actions. Like friendship, good teaching is not something that can be entirely scripted, preplanned, or prespecified. If a person is thoughtful, caring, and committed, mistakes will be made, but they will not be disastrous; if a person lacks commitment, compassion, or thought, outstanding technique and style will never really compensate. Teaching is primarily a matter of love. The rest is, at best, ornamentation, nice to look at but not of the essence; at worst it is obfuscating—it pulls our attention in the wrong direction and turns us away from the heart of the matter. (18)

Students, rather than curriculum, are the heart of the matter. Ayers' teaching experience led him to believe "the curriculum had the same general relationship to knowledge or understanding as McDonald's has to nutrition" (88). He suggests that we abandon the practice of starting with what students don't know, and concentrate on what students do know. Since lesson plans are typically built around what students don't know, "we must find ways to break with the deficit-driven models, and we must move away from teaching as a way of attacking incompetencies, teaching as uncovering perceived deficiencies and constructing micro-units for repair" (32).

Ayers' own careful and consistent observations of children, well related throughout his memoir, provide him with insight and inspiration, not with objectivity. He claims that it is impossible to construct an objective record of any student. "The goal of observation is understanding, not some imagined objectivity" (37). Parents, according to Ayers, are yet another "powerful, usually underutilized source of knowledge about youngsters" (39) available to teachers, but the students themselves by far remain the strongest source of knowledge. "I reject the idea that learning is passive, that the teacher is the 'one who knows,' and the students are the 'ones who don't know'" (57).

Ayers denigrates standardized testing. His own experience taking a standardized test for a teaching certificate was frustrating and depressing. "Teaching never seemed so silly, so empty, so worthless. And yet, according to the state, if I passed the test, I would now be qualified and ready to teach. That part of the experience made me furious" (114). But what standardized testing does not measure is even more frustrating and depressing for Ayers. "After all, standardized tests can't measure initiative, creativity, imagination, conceptual thinking, curiosity, effort, irony, judgment, commitment, nuance, good will, ethical reflection, or a host of other valuable dispositions and attributes" (116). "Standardized tests," he sums up, "should come with printed warnings: USE OF THESE MATERIALS MAY BE HAZARDOUS TO YOUR INTELLIGENCE, or THE LIFE CHANCES OF HALF OF THOSE TAKING THESE TESTS WILL BE NARROWED" (119). Instead, he favors projects, performances, and portfolios as alternative, more effective methods of evaluation. Committed to these methods of evaluation, Ayers not only uses them in his elementary school teaching, but also in seminars he leads for aspiring teachers.

For example, in my seminar for teachers we discuss classroom issues regularly, we work on a wide variety of complex concerns, and we range over a lot of densely covered ground. And in the end, each student presents a portfolio that includes: a learning agenda, a pedagogical autobiography, a description of core teaching values, a letter to the author of a self-selected, published teacher autobiography, a child study, a brief philosophy of education, a self-evaluation, a recollection of outstanding moments as a student, a description of a failed teaching attempt, a review of a self-selected autobiography of childhood, a practical art, and a revised learning agenda or action plan for the immediate future. This portfolio leaves a lot out, of course, but it also reflects and emphasizes qualities I value in teaching. (124)

Having the strength and passion of a manifesto, Ayers' memoir ultimately identifies teaching as mystery. Drawing on the innovations of Konstantin Stanislavsky, Ayers suggests that good teaching, like great acting, engages audiences, interacts with them, and draws energy and inspiration from the relationship. It also requires a serious encounter with autobiography. Teachers must reach inside themselves and summon up particular aspects of their own knowledge and experience in order to teach well.

Since Ayers' own teaching experience has been in public elementary schools, he never makes reference to Catholic schools. However, what his manifesto calls for—community over institution—is at the heart of successful contemporary Catholic schools.

Even though we long for community—for places of common vision, shared purpose, cooperative effort, and personal fulfillment within collective commitment—we most often settle for institutions. That is, we generally find ourselves in impersonal places characterized by interchangeable parts, hierarchy, competition, and layers of supervision. Communities have problems and possibilities; schools and universities have departments. We are reduced to clerks or bureaucrats, and our sense of purpose and agency is diminished. (64–65)

Certainly Catholic schools are not educational utopias, but the post–Vatican Council II emphasis on community as an essential mark of church has invigorated many Catholic schools, nurtured the vocation of teachers, and fostered an environment in which that vocation can flourish.

Ayers' memoir manifesto establishes an extraordinarily person-centered perspective and solution to our schooling dilemmas. He believes it is not mechanistic organization or efficient management alone that will ultimately quell our educational nightmares. Only the teacher who is deeply in contact with a spirituality of education, living it out with students in a supportive environment, will bring a good night's sleep to the nation.

Reflective Exercises

❖ What events in your life do you spend a lot of time thinking about?

❖ Where do you do your best in-depth thinking about your own life?

❖ What have been some "confessional moments" in your own life?

❖ What life stories have given you the feeling of "being there" or "standing in another's shoes" when you hear or read them?

❖ Have you ever yearned for good conversation? When have you felt this yearning lately? What was it like? What led to it? What did you do?

❖ Recall a stimulating discussion that engaged your mind and heart. Are there certain people in your past or present with whom you have these conversations regularly? What do these discussions do for you?

❖ How do you nurture your spirit? through retreats? books? relationships? spiritual direction? rituals?

❖ Focusing on one specific incident, recall your best teacher. What made this person the best?

❖ Recall the most miserable point of your educational experience. What happened? What did you learn from this?

❖ How would you describe your philosophy of education? What educational experiences influenced your ideas?

5

Reading Memoirs; Writing Memoirs

Introduction

The expanding availability of knowledge coupled with the decreasing number of citizens who can avail themselves of information through various forms of literacy is a significant concern for contemporary culture. Yet death knells for reading and eulogies for writing are premature and overdone.[1] Electronic media has no more driven a fatal stake into the heart of the written word than literacy has annihilated speech. This age of electronic media, however, does situate the written word in an arena vastly different from the world before film, television, and the computer. Reading is no longer the singular gateway to information and wisdom; no longer is the book the primary mode of delivery. Writing is no longer the singular purveyor of information and wisdom; no longer are words on paper the exclusive mode of delivery.

Happily, despite rumors to the contrary, reading and writing are here to stay. Some suggest that books now bound in volumes will increasingly appear on computer screens and then be transferred to hard copy by printers. Although that might be the fate of highly technical books with extraordinarily limited audiences, my suspicion is that texts with wide appeal will be readily available in the familiar bound format for many years to come. Megabookstores increasingly lure people into the world of reading. Thousands of books are published annually in the United States. The sheer volume of new books indicates an enormous market for the written word.

Writing not only survives but thrives. Computers permit students to easily write and edit their work and, in the opinion of some teachers, have begun to turn the tide of poor writing into a resurgence of competence and creativity.

Separating the Wheat from the Chaff

Writers learn their craft in part by reading. The traditional guide for determining what is worthwhile reading is a canon. Canons, be they religious or secular, public or private, represent matters determined, fixed by some authority, and therefore appear unchangeable. A canon is a "standard of judgement or authority; a test, criterion, means of discrimination."[2] Literary canons are other people's or other group's determinations of what is most worth reading. The concept and the practice favor the classical over the contemporary, the time-tested over the current or the immediately relevant, the established over the prophetic, and the Eurocultural over the multicultural.

Traditional canons offer limited sources for would-be memoir readers to consult. As has been pointed out, memoir eschews classical categories of knowledge, avoids attempts at universalization, gives voice to the heretofore voiceless in many societies and cultures, and often functions as a prophetic voice within a culture. The contemporaneity of many memoirs also militates against inclusion in canons.

The lack of congruity between memoir and canon testifies to the diverse nature of the genre. How then might someone interested in memoir find guidance and direction in such a sea of diversity? I think, rather than looking to official canons, the nature of the genre suggests people look toward establishing a more personal canon. Just as memoir's source of authority is personal, so too are the best sources of memoir.

Repositories of the Written Word

As even a casual visitor notices, a contemporary megabookstore with its easy chairs and desks available for readers to peruse inexpensively priced volumes, and, often a coffeehouse as part of the premises, reflects more than aggressive marketing. These bookstores inspire almost like cathedrals. The inspiration comes not only from the books available for purchase, but also from the many and varied people who come to peruse and to purchase books. This environment both nurtures and stimulates the imagination.

Regretfully, operators of small bookstores find it impossible to stock such a wide array of books or to price books competitively, and are often unable to afford the luxurious environment that megabookstores provide their customers. Yet many owners of these small bookstores are themselves compendiums of knowledge, virtually walking and talking libraries. They are an endangered species in the reality of today's economic marketplace.

Libraries are yet another testimony to reading. Whether it is the stateliness of the Harold Washington Library in downtown Chicago, one of the largest city libraries in the world, or the intimacy of the San Juan Capistrano library in southern California, these buildings speak of something important happening within their confines. Hospitable librarians anxiously want to be helpful. One librarian in the Chicago area, in imitation of the contemporary combinations of bookstores and coffeehouses, has started to serve refreshments to library patrons.

Such activity and interest in books indicates that, like Mark Twain's reported death, the announced death of literacy is premature. Amid the many tomes, hundreds of memoirs stand cheek by jowl with the incredible manifestation of literacy carried on bookstore and library shelves.

Locating Worthwhile Memoirs

How to choose worthwhile memoirs? This question, especially significant in light of the plethora of available memoirs published today, leads to selectivity, not randomness, as crucial to the process. Just because a text gets called "a memoir" does not certify its integrity. As has been mentioned already, scam memoirs, hastily written to turn a profit, are not icons of experience nor do they depict or present serious and substantial reflection on life experiences and events.

Book reviews, bookstores, libraries, and people who read with discrimination and sensitivity are invaluable resources identifying and locating worthwhile memoirs.

Many major newspapers include a daily book review in addition to a weekly book review section, usually as part of a weekend edition. Book reviews, of course, represent only a fragment of published books, and then offer only one person's opinion. Whether a book is reviewed or not, and what the individual reviewer chooses to write about it is extraordinarily subjective. Nonetheless, book reviews are a valuable resource for identifying possible worthwhile memoirs.

Bookstores offer another valuable introduction to memoir. Bookstores that display their wares attractively, encourage browsing, and have literate and knowledgeable people behind their counters are great resources. The memoir treasures are often shelved in a variety of categories of nonfiction. The diligent seeker of worthwhile memoir, therefore, needs to peruse many nonfiction sections and even many fiction sections.

College and university bookstores are another great place to browse for memoirs. One has to make one's way through ever increasing hoards of T-shirts, sweatshirts, nightshirts, jackets, stuffed animals, coats, pennants, blankets, canvas bags, glasses, steins, mugs, salt and pepper shakers, and just about anything else that can be embroidered or stamped with the school's logo and sport school colors. When one finally reaches the section of the store where books are arranged by department and individual course, memoirs may be discovered. Since teachers from many disciplines assign memoirs as either required or recommended reading in various courses, a search of these shelves frequently yields interesting and provocative titles.

Used-book stores are also valuable depositories for serious and substantial memoirs. Some of these stores have little or no organization, a hodgepodge of books stacked hither and yon. They are fine for people with archaeological tendencies who relish searching for important shreds and shards in a lot of dirt. Other used-book stores yield their treasures more readily.

Browsing for memoirs in libraries can be more confining than surveying bookstores. In many cases library budgets limit their acquisitions. However, libraries, like the good used-book store, outdistance new bookstores in older memoirs and out-of-print books. Libraries networked into interlibrary loan services multiply their "holdings" often by millions of books and add almost infinite resources for informed readers.

My own best source of identifying worthwhile memoirs is other people. Friends, associates, former and present students—all who read widely and well—are better than the best book review section of a newspaper, better than the best bookstore, and better than the best library. A recommendation from someone I know personally and whose judgment I admire moves that book to the top of my list. Frequently I'll take the initiative, asking friends, "What good books have you read recently?" And I'm always prepared to share two or three recent books that impressed me. Some of their recommendations, of course, are memoirs.

Mining Worthwhile Memoirs

Reading a memoir, like reading other worthwhile forms of literature, is a highly participatory and relational activity involving the interaction among three distinct though related entities: the reader, the author, and the text.

The author, by writing a memoir, has created a work of art. The reader encounters this artistic product, an icon of experience, and begins to form a relationship with it. This relationship is both similar to and different from the encounter with visual art—a painting or a piece of sculpture. With written memoir, the totality of the work is experienced only after the last page is turned, the last word read. Visual art usually places its totality immediately before a person, and it is the art in its entirety that makes the initial impression. Texts reveal themselves page by page, and readers, often within the first few pages, establish an initial relationship with the text. This initial relationship often determines the pattern by which a reader will view the text. Some people quickly stop reading if they fail to sense a satisfying relationship developing. Other readers are more patient, reading more pages or chapters before deciding to continue or to dismiss the unfolding relationship with a particular manuscript.

By means of memoir the writer invites the reader into a particular world, allows the reader to walk around in it, participate in it, and, ultimately, learn something about and from these presented experiences. The artistry employed in a specific memoir, the subject matter, and the reader's reaction to the subject matter facilitate or deter this relational process as well. A particular memoir's subject matter may simply not interest some readers. Other subject matter might be so painful for certain readers that they choose not to continue reading.

Reading, some say, should be enjoyable. I would prefer to emphasize the experience of reading, especially the experience of reading memoirs, as satisfying. Some of the greatest works of literature, both classical, like *Oedipus Rex*[3] or the tragedies of Shakespeare, and contemporary, like Elie Wiesel's Holocaust writings,[4] deal with horrible subject matter. They are not enjoyable to read, but they do satisfy.

They open windows filled with insight and wisdom on the world of humanity. Certain memoirs do this too. The subject matter might not be particularly pleasant to read about, but the wisdom that memoirists share about painful experiences can be satisfying for readers.

Intelligent and sensitive memoir reading is guided by the artistry of memoir as well as by its highly relational and participatory nature. Helpful guidelines and usable guideposts to memoir reading rest on these internal qualities. Unlike Mortimer Adler and Charles Van Doren's *How to Read a Book,*[5] which orients readers toward an analytical and dissectional approach and does not even mention memoir as a book form, I prefer an approach that respects the artistry of the text and fosters the relationality among text, author, and reader.

Such an approach puts a great deal of emphasis on the reader's ability to encounter and interact with texts as art forms. Developing an appreciation for the transrational artistry of words is sometimes difficult and seemingly at odds with the perceived intentionality of words. Words in combination are art forms. Poetry communicates this reality well, but so too does good prose. Whether it is the effusive prose of Thomas Wolfe or James Agee, the highly descriptive prose of Charles Dickens or John Irving, or the crisp prose of Ernest Hemingway or Barbara Kingsolver, art created by word usage is integral and intimate to what authors write about and to the impression they want to make on the reader.

The art established by an author's use of words becomes either a gateway or a barrier to the text. Readers who have developed appreciative skills in art and then transfer these skills to an appreciation of the artistry of language, therefore, tend to read memoirs well.

Samuel Taylor Coleridge, perhaps best remembered for "The Rime of the Ancient Mariner," writes about "the willing suspension of disbelief."[6] Memoir readers sometimes need to willingly suspend their disbelief, too. As one enters into another's experience through created memoir, an openness to, rather than judgment of, this new and different world view is essential. By suspending disbelief and shelving suspicion, readers enter the world of the icon, not with aggression but with curiosity. This curiosity motivates readers to look carefully at the details of the story, to consider where the author is coming from and going to, and to eventually reflect on the circumstances and the significances of the story. Careful writers, like good visual artists, leave no details unattended; neither should readers.

Encountering another person's presence, observing another person's world, learning another person's point of view are sacred activities. Moses removed his shoes on such holy ground, as did Mrs. Moore when she first entered a mosque in E. M. Forster's *A Passage to India*.[7] Readers should approach and participate in memoir like other sacred activity, with reverence—not timid, pious reverence but robust, energized reverence. Reading reverently makes demands, but gently and intimately.

Certain memoirs do not lend themselves to such generosity. Adolph Hitler's *Mein Kampf*,[8] the memoir and manifesto of his early life, for example, or Charles Manson's book *Manson in His Own Words*[9] challenge anyone to extend such courtesy. Even these memoirs, however, create a world that allows readers to encounter, walk around in, and learn from these two twisted people. This of course is a judgment. But when readers turn the last page of a memoir, they eventually do judge, that is, they reach an evaluation of the wisdom ultimately put forth by the text.

Judgment is one goal of reading memoir. Coming to judgment follows no neat pattern, but generally people do this by comparing and contrasting the encountered wisdom of a memoir with other sources of wisdom, their personal experiences, the collected wisdom of given cultural mores, and the given wisdom of various religious traditions. Just as memoirists write from their personal point of view and the culture in which they live, readers judge the wisdom of a memoir from the point of view of their experience and culture. Just as memoirs are not created in a vacuum, neither are they read in a vacuum. Readers bring their whole self, culture and religious tradition included, to the enterprise.

Perhaps the best benchmark for judging the worthwhileness of a memoir is not in how it stands up under analytical scrutiny or rigorous research-oriented probing. Rather, these questions might prove more useful: Does a memoir capture your imagination and interest long after having read it? Are you still thinking about it weeks and months later? Do you find yourself telling other people about it? Have you entered passages from it in your Book of Commonplace? If readers answer yes to these questions, the memoir has become a benchmark for them.

Writing Memoirs

Looking back over the various forms and styles of memoir, starting with gutturals and proceeding to artistic product, many practical and useful methodologies emerge. Some are specific and to the point; others are more long range and probing. All are useful.

One of the best preparations for writing memoirs, of course, is reading worthwhile memoirs well. The styles and forms, though diverse, lend themselves to imitation. Encountering an artistic text that aptly captures life experiences and richly reflects on their signficances has often been the triggering event for another memoirist. Good memoirs inspire and encourage others to go and do likewise.

Exorcising Censor Demons

Many memoirists have some demon censors that need exorcising before they write. Putting pen to paper or putting disk in computer stymies some people. Images of stern English teachers flunking students for one misspelled word, one out-of-place punctuation mark, or a lone dangling modifier freeze them. The self-revelation and introspection that writing about oneself engenders pose another stumbling block for some people. Couple the two—writing and writing about one's own life—and paralysis besets would-be memoirists.

Writing and writing about oneself, fortunately, have become more acceptable in this therapeutic age and thus less threatening. The grammatical method of teaching writing has given way to other methods of instruction that focus on one's inner energy and that encourage creative expression. The formalities of grammar, spelling, and punctuation, although important and necessary, are left to the latter stages of the writing process.

Learning from the Children

In many schools today, children from the earliest grades express themselves through the written word, especially in journals that become more than daily assignments but portfolios of all kinds of expression. Children publish class newspapers, write found poems, chain poems, and autobiographies.

One specific methodology uses a form of poem to create a brief memoir. William Ayers, in his memoir *To Teach: The Journey of a Teacher*,[10] asks students to quickly compose a short poem about themselves. They complete the first line, "I am . . . ," with their first name; the next line needs to have three self-describing words; the next line begins with "I love . . .," followed by a line beginning with "I hate . . ." The next two lines begin with "I am afraid . . ." and "I wish for . . ." The last line is simply the student's surname. One such poem, in just thirty words, communicates a wealth of memoir in this young child's brief life:

> I am Aaron
>   small, black, frightened
>   I love my mom
>   I hate being picked on
>   I am afraid of the raper man and the police
>   I wish for happiness
> Blackwell.[11]

This technique also works well with adults. I suspect that it does so because it begins to touch on memoir through a deceptively simple exercise that produces an immediate icon of experience.

Adults can start writing their memoirs by learning from children: start with day-to-day experience, write what you know, keep it short, make it playful, and forget anyone might read it.

Journal

Ultimately people learn to write by writing, and one extraordinarily helpful way of writing, especially for a would-be memoirist, is journaling. Many excellent books provide both less-structured and highly structured approaches to journal keeping.

Natalie Goldberg in *Writing Down the Bones*[12] and Christina Baldwin in *Life's Companion: Journal Writing as a Spiritual Quest*[13] both offer scores of ways to start writing in a journal. Goldberg, Baldwin, and other journal-keepers typically suggest techniques such as the following to get started:

The timed exercise. Timed writing encourages people to express themselves by initially setting aside form and structure. People engaged in this exercise write continuously for a period of time: five, ten, fifteen minutes, or longer. They do not concern themselves with grammar, spelling, or punctuation. They record on paper whatever comes into their mind. Natalie Goldberg offers six practical suggestions to practitioners of this exercise: (1) Keep your hand moving; (2) Don't cross out; (3) Don't worry about spelling, punctuation, grammar; (4) Lose control; (5) Don't think. Don't get logical; and (6) Go for the jugular.[14]

Flow writing. "Flow writing is practice in stream of consciousness, learning to trust that no matter where you start, words will come to you."[15] Christina Baldwin recommends that journal writers pick an object in the place where they are and let it trigger writing. As with timed writing, the journal writer plunges in and starts writing, letting the mind free-associate while writing down whatever comes to mind.

By following these two disciplines regularly, freeing aspects of writing emerge in the form of first thoughts. These first thoughts have tremendous energy and are unencumbered by ego. After these first thoughts are out of the self and on to the page, then people can begin to work with them further.

Dialog writing. In some ways, all writing is a dialog between the writer and a question—an unsolved conflict with an experience from the past or a person who played a significant role in the writer's life. Writing carries on these conversations. Writing dialogs helps journal-keepers more consciously converse with events, questions, people, and even their body. While writing a dialog, writers put themselves in the other person's shoes. They play both roles, thus expanding their perception and range of feeling.

The simplest way to begin a dialog is to ask a question. For instance, journal-keepers and memoirists might want to recapture their early disgust with their body-self. They could start the dialog with their body by asking: "Body, what was it like for you back when I was boy [or girl]? How did you feel about yourself?" Once the question is asked, the response is recorded and the dialog continues.

To kindle images and memories of people important in the past, dialog writing can also be helpful. The conversation might begin with these questions: How come you never praised my accomplishments when I was a kid? What did those fishing trips mean to you? You hated your job, so why did you stay with it so long? Once the question is asked, the dialog continues like any conversation.

The journal-keeper and memoirist can dialog with any thing or any person. Christina Baldwin concludes that "dialogue is the most versatile tool of journal writing. We can avoid looking directly at issues for a long time while writing in monologue, but dialogue gets to the heart of the matter."[16]

Timed writing, flow writing, and dialog writing are only three of the techniques that journal-keepers and memoirists can use to plunge into their experiences, their memories, their lives. These less-structured approaches have immense value. People have also found highly structured journal keeping to be invaluable as they move toward memoir writing.

The Intensive Journal

The Intensive Journal developed by Ira Progoff has an interesting origin. After serving in the army in World War II, Ira Progoff returned home to consider the possible effect of the Nazi agenda on the world if they had successfully destroyed all sacred scriptures and books of wisdom through their activity of ritual book burning.

This consideration led Progoff to two insights. First, he was impressed with the human spirit as a vast, self-replenishing resource that could not be annihilated, even though manifestations of the spirit found in books of sacred scriptures and other wisdom books could be destroyed. Second, he also was impressed with humanity's ability to arrive at additional spiritual insights from the depths of experience. "Taken jointly, these new 'bibles' of interior wisdom can be perceived as a saga of spiritual unfoldment among many persons in the modern era," writes James P. Armstrong of Ira Progoff and his Intensive Journal. He continues, "Progoff considers the creation of individual 'scriptures', and the meaning in the traditional ones, as essential to the further qualitative evolution of humankind."[17]

Ira Progoff's Intensive Journal workshops experientially introduce participants to a structured form of journal keeping. His book *At a Journal Workshop* is the basic text for Progoff's entire system that underpins his series of workshops.[18] Other workshops, Process Meditation, Depth Psychology, and Life Study, further the basic process. The journal, a notebook divided into twenty-five specific parts, provides structure to record experiences and events from one's life and to reflect on their signficances. "Each section is used with specific active procedures that serve to evoke the contents of a person's life without analysis or diagnosis, but in such a way as to stimulate additional inner perceptions and movements of many kinds."[19]

Progoff's Life Study workshop and process is particularly fascinating. A participant becomes a journal trustee for some other person who lived previously. By using the Intensive Journal method, the participant enters into the inner world of the chosen person. This experience is akin to that of the sacred biographers of the Middle Ages who preserved not the externals of saints' lives, but the inner dynamics of their experiences.

The Progoff Intensive Journal workshop provides participants with a structure and a method for writing. It also gives them triggering activities that release inner energy to fund the process of journaling. Additionally, the experience of a Progoff workshop inspires and motivates many participants to continue their journaling process long after the workshop ends. The twenty-five sections of an Intensive Journal provide memoirists with a rich mine for writing memoir.

Fictive Writing

Fiction, as has been already pointed out, is yet another mode of expression for communicating life experiences, events, and their significances. Erving Polster, author of *Every Person's Life Is Worth a Novel,* and a therapist of forty years, is dismayed by how uninteresting most psychological writing is.[20] Most of it, according to Polster, fails to capture the "fascinating nature of people's lives or how salutary it is for patients to feel this quality in themselves."[21] His stated goal in the preface to this book is to unite therapy with the healing recognition that accompanies the realization that all people's lives are truly fascinating. "No model for this union could serve my purposes better than that of the novelist, with whom the therapist has a kinship in the deep exploration of human behavior and awareness."[22]

Conclusion

Reading and writing are two sides of the same coin. Although cultural obstacles deter people from serious reading, happily many people, places, and things promote it. Serious readers must take the initiative to link themselves with available sources and resources for worthwhile reading. This is especially true for readers of memoir because the contemporary manifestations of this genre are both nascent and myriad.

Although reading is excellent preparation for writing, many readers still hesitate to write. Fortunately, many methodologies encourage and foster good writing today. Many of these are uniquely suited to memoir because exploration of personal experience is at the heart of these exercises and methodologies.

Memoir is a participatory event. It relies on people who are willing and able to express themselves successfully. Energy, dedication, and discipline are foundations for such authorship.

"Extra Innings": A Reflection

I cringe at the oft voiced idea that sports are a metaphor for life. Is this because I perceive myself better at life than at sports? Is this because I harbor the suspicion that sports fanatics believe it the opposite: life is a metaphor for sports? Nonetheless, I became intrigued with Doris Grumbach's book's primal metaphor, its title, *Extra Innings* (New York: W. W. Norton, 1993).

Why a woman of decidedly feminist character titles her most recent book with a distinctively male, sports-oriented phrase is but one intrigue of *Extra Innings*. Doesn't this title clash with feminism? Here is a woman, for example, who writes about leaving the Catholic church some years ago "because of its inexcusable treatment of women" (28). Hardly the stuff of sports jargon. Veteran Grumbach readers, however, might not be so surprised by her title rhetoric since her earlier memoir, *Coming into the End Zone*, also plays off another metaphor of a typically male sport.[23]

People who do not appreciate the deliberately subtle aura of baseball think an extra-inning game cruel and unusual punishment. For baseball aficionados who follow and sometimes carefully record the incredible nuances in every move of the game, extra innings become both a *kairos,* a moment of opportunity, and a hierophany, a manifestation of the sacred.

Doris Grumbach approaches her own life much the same way the serious, knowledgeable, appreciative lover of baseball relates to the sport. Every nuance counts mightily. She captures this relationship by retelling what Simon, a character in a Padgett Powell novel, says: "'This is my motto: Never to forget that, dull as things get, old as it is, something's happening, happening all the time, and to watch it'"(40). Among the things happening in her own life are the loss of contact with old friends, books, relocation from Washington, D.C., to rural Maine, good and not-so-good book reviews, testimonial dinners, informal get-togethers in Manhattan, the possible life-threatening illness of her now adult child, travels away from home and then returns home, more books, bookstores, gathering for church, and visitors to her rural homeland.

For her, the stuff of a given day or, by extension, a given year reveals a venerability about living and a sacredness about life. She is somewhere on that spectrum of old, older, or oldest age; only her death will mark with certitude what spot on the spectrum of geriatric life she now lives and writes about. Toward that end she ponders: "Perhaps dying is like this: walking, without stopping, into absolute, complete, silent fog toward an inscrutable clearing at the end" (236).

Doris Grumbach published her first reflections on the latter part of life at seventy years of age when she wrote *Coming into the End Zone*, a book about entering her seventies and the accompanying feelings of desperation. Nearly five years later she published a similar milepost memoir of experience and wisdom.

> I have chosen to follow the same journal-jotting procedure I used four years ago. Perhaps, in the process of writing, I may come upon some answers to the insistent questions of old age. Or perhaps I will only succeed in recording, month by month, the minor thoughts and activities in the life of an aging woman. It may be that a commonplace record of insignificant exterior doings and interior musings *are* my only possible response to the great philosophical questions. What is it that drives us to examine matters of cosmic significance—birth, faith, suffering, injustice, dying, and death—but the intrusion into our daily lives of niggling irritations and petty trifles. (9)

Memoirs take different tacks. Some reach far back into time to examine a particular period in one's life. Others plumb a single dramatic event. The span of time separating experiences from the recollection of them gives many memoirists the luxury to reflect for years upon the meaning of their life and the leisure to record it just right. Doris Grumbach does not give herself such luxury or leisure. *Extra Innings* records everyday events shortly after they happen.

Perhaps it need be so in later life when such a time lag quite possibly might not be available. But there is yet another reason for such memoir-making. After long years spent thinking deeply about life experiences, one is able to read almost instantaneously the deep and explicit significance of life events. This is true of *Extra Innings*.

Grumbach knows the inner dynamics of memoir writing and shares them willingly with her readers:

> Writing one memoir, and then taking these notes for another, I am struck by the dubiousness of the whole enterprise of autobiography. The words "truth" and "fact" keep insinuating themselves into every entry I make and into the reviews that have begun to

arrive from Gerry Howard. The more I think about what I have written, and about what I am writing now, the clearer becomes what Blanche Boyd once wrote, I think, about Norman Mailer: "Everything is altered by the observer." At the moment of retrieval, in the process of recall the initial, observer-limited memory is there, incomplete and biased as it was when first it was stored in the mind. Then it is embroidered and encrusted over time (I think of the Ladies of Llangollen's eighteenth-century house in Wales that was replaced in the next century with Tudor brown wood and "improved," thus changing the original cottage forever) until it is like a barnacle-covered shell, with little of the original shape to be seen.

Then I write about it, giving the memory a literary shape. I leave out what no longer pleases my view of myself. I embellish with euphony and decorate the prose with some color. I subordinate, giving less importance to some matters, raising others to the weight of coordination. I modify. During this literary activity that surrounds the "germ" of fact, as Henry James called it, I am moving into, well, *style,* and away from, well, let's face it, truth. But I persist, driven by the need to record in readable form what I think about and remember, however unreliable. (14–15)

For some people, explanation of memoir-making might be like a magician revealing how magic tricks work. Yet Grumbach's reflections on her writing life, writing about her own life, and others writing about their life are strong, clear, worthwhile, and challenging. She is supportive of people who desire to write their memoirs. She maintains that "everyone who has lived for a while has within them wonderful memories, events that only they are privy to" (71). One person, married many times, has another motivation. Grumbach quotes her, "'I'll be eighty this month. Age, if nothing else, entitles me to set the record straight before I dissolve. I've given my memoirs far more thought than any of my marriages. You can't divorce a book'" (127).

Writers, particularly memoir writers, perhaps unknowingly reveal more than they plan. Grumbach knows the transparency of the writing process, and comments on it:

It *is* curious to read books written by friends or acquaintances, especially if they are autobiographical, and to realize how little one has really known about the writers, how much one has been unable even to guess about them. Finding their lives fixed strangely

to the page by their own hand is something like being in a for-
eign city and coming upon a married friend from home accompanied by a lady not his wife. Shock. Why is he here? Who is
she? What is going on? How is it I never guessed? Did I really
know him at all? Truly, we know almost nothing about each other, no matter how close or closely related we are, and what we
think we know often turns out to be mistaken. (33–34)

But Grumbach knows that many people who talk about writing memoirs will never do it. She finds the usual "if I only had the time" ex-
cuse annoying. The comment, to her way of thinking, defines a writer
as "someone who is not doing something more important, like them,
and therefore has the time" (71).

Another caveat Grumbach assigns to memoir-making is a painful
one. Attention to and reflection on everything has its downside.
Grumbach describes this:

Keeping a journal thins my skin. I feel open to everything, aware,
charged by the acquisition of interesting (to me) entries, hyper-
sensitive to whatever I hear, see, guess, read, am told. Matters
that once might have gone unnoticed are no longer lost on me. I
may sue my publisher for not providing me with sufficient pro-
tection against assault by whatever sensations are out there. (90)

Memoir-making, in spite of its downside, is a worthwhile activity
for Doris Grumbach. She is like the person sitting in the grandstand of
a baseball park, pencil sharpened, recording every play, and thereby
maintaining relational intimacy with the action. Her attention to every
detail of the extra innings of her life creates a memoir worth reading
and, for some, worth emulating. Her many and worthwhile reflections
on journal keeping, the act of writing, and memoir-making, in addition to being highly accurate, also inspire. The would-be writer of
memoir will get both practical insight and powerful inspiration from
this memoir.

"The Last Farmer": A Reflection

This memoir disturbingly suggests that a center point of our national mythology is irreversibly close to death. It disturbs, even though not since the early 1900s has the majority of the country's population lived in rural areas. It disturbs, even though the farm family climbing county courthouse steps on their way to a farm foreclosure hearing or standing in front of the homestead as the farm gets auctioned out from under their feet have been commonplace clips on newscasts. It disturbs, even though family farms now make up decreasing portions of farmland in this country. *The Last Farmer,* by Howard Kohn (New York: Harper and Row, 1989), is a creatively disturbing memoir.

Keeper of the land, supplier of food, harbinger of hard work, the farmer symbolizes much that is noble in the American tradition (used car salespeople, junk bond dealers, and fat cat corporate CEOs envy, though hardly emulate, the farmer). Cradle of the country, progenitor of food, breadbasket of the world, the farm, more specifically, the family farm, is the site of much that is noble in the American tradition (gentrified neighborhoods, public parks, and fashionable suburbs pale by comparison).

The farm is sacred space, akin to chapels and cathedrals, where urban and suburban folks temporarily migrate to second homes, to weekends in the country, to farm vacations. Urban and suburban people press close to this center of our national consciousness, to rest, to reflect, to retire, indeed, to pray.

By comparison, his high school diploma fresh in hand, in the prime of adolescence, Howard Kohn shook the dust of his Michigan farm from his feet and, like so many of the rural born population, left: left for college, left for the city, the big city, the Big Apple, New York. And now, in midlife, on top of a successful writing career (Kohn is the author of *Who Killed Karen Silkwood?*[24]), he returns home, accompanied by his second wife, to confront and to comfort his family, his father, his own faith, all inseparable though dissonant, all centered on that mighty and mysterious piece of land, the family farm.

I was not only another runaway, but, as someone wantonly and hugely malcontent, I was the flipside of my father. Where he was rooted in the earth, I was on the loose and on the make. And each day I was away from the farm, the more incomprehensible my father's life seemed to me. Even in the indirect, biblical sense, what was it?—really no more than a delaying action. Sooner or later some big, rich farmer would take over the Kohn land in synchrony with the larger twentieth-century appetite for acquisitions and economic cannibalism which, let the arbitragers teach us, is at once the spirit of the American dream and the essence of one generation's superiority over the last one. If my father had been at all predatory, grabbing land when neighbors died, he might have had a fighting chance, but, on his one hundred and twenty acres, he was in a state—of ennui? of hiding from the real world? or quailing before it?—of having a total disregard, at any rate, for bettering himself, so it seemed to me. He represented the great romanticized myth of the American farmer, trying to survive on his terms no matter what. I knew the myth, of course, and I had marveled at it, been staggered by it, but I had never believed it. (17–18)

Echoes of the prodigal son reverberate, yet *The Last Farmer* is a far more detailed story. It is a thick description of rural living, family farming in the latter half of the twentieth century, the father-son relationship, midlife crisis, and more. As the author wrestles with the possibility of permanently returning to the family farm, home of his ailing, aging father, Fredrick, home of his deceased ancestors, grandfather Johann and great-grandfather Heinrich, he confronts far more than the management of these one hundred and twenty acres of earth in Beaver Township, Michigan.

So, to echo Wordsworth, is the child father of the man? Howard Kohn, as he ponders whether or not to stand in his father's boots on the land farmed by three generations of Kohns, comes to a new awareness of his father's life, his own chosen vocation, and the relationship between the two. "I fully realized how much my writing is like my father's farming and how much I had become like my father. Writing and farming are endeavors of the solitary, driven soul, driving against the odds" (257).

Kohn's memoir separates the ideals embodied in rural lifeways from geographical proximity to the land. Living on the land is not essential to living a life imbued with values that underpin the American family farm mythology. Nor does geography alone determine fidelity to one's family or faith.

The Last Farmer poses a somewhat harsh and decidedly difficult challenge for the majority of people in this country. It challenges urbanites and suburbanites to quit thinking that a quick weekend in the country is in itself the gateway to virtue, to begin living the values embedded in our agrarian mythology, not superficially through get-away weekends, but substantially in the midst of urban and suburban culture.

Howard Kohn's father models such behavior for us all when he decides to sell the family farm, not to the highest bidder, a mineral company willing to rape the land by exploration, but to a lower bidder who will continue to reverence the land through farming (imagine what a revolution such behavior might engender in the often spiraling prices of urban real estate).

> And it is enough, I realize now, more than enough, when you have kept a deep sense of yourself. Character is all that any of us have at the end, the sole property that is ours. I don't mean to rationalize. My father loved his farm, but he understood better than I the ironies implicit in passing on a farm in your own image. The land mocks the farmer by outlasting him and outlasting his family, no matter the number of successive generations. The one thing of permanence that a farmer can bequeath—a life of respect and respectful virtues—will be rendered ironic and pathetic if he begins to act as if he is entitled to a bailout, whether from the government or from his children. My father had to work at understanding this. It was not given. It was an achievement, like any work. I had thought of Heinrich as a pioneer, going off to a new land, and I had thought of my father as a stand-pat guy. But it was my father who had geared himself up for the bold stroke, who saw that the farm did not hold us together, as I had thought, but stood between him and his children. So he sold it and brought us back together, or rather had gone off to find us, all of us in our own places. (269–270)

This is not an easy end to the story. Readers looking for a superficial, romantic sweep back into the past, akin to a weekend in the country, might be disappointed. Readers willing to be challenged in their own time and space by the spirituality of the American mythology, represented by but not solely incarnated in the family farm, will be challenged by Howard Kohn's "American memoir."

Reflective Exercises

❖ What books have you received as gifts that have been important in your life? What books have you given as gifts that you wanted to be important in other people's lives?

❖ Recall both difficult and satisfying experiences of writing in your life. What made them difficult, satisfying, or both?

❖ Recall all the blessings that have been significant in your life. Name each one. Take a step further and tell the story of each blessing. To get into practice, try to keep a "Blessing-a-Day" log in your journal for the next couple of weeks.

❖ Using the same process as you did for logging your blessings, recollect your "Crises History."

❖ Write a dialog with someone from your childhood or teenage years who has passed out of your life, but whose influence remains. Start the dialog with a question that you would like to ask now, looking back.

❖ Grumbach was living her extra innings. Many of us never dream as children that we will live the life that we ultimately do. Write a dialog with the child you were at ten years of age, beginning with the questions: "What do you think you will be when you grow up? What kind of life will you have?"

❖ Have another talk with the child you were, but this time at age sixteen. Talk about your body-self back then. Start with a question about a body issue that you had then, that has stayed with you, or that you have now.

❖ Flow write or do a timed writing, using as your starting point one of these themes: forgiveness, trust, acceptance, love, want, belief, power, fear.

❖ Write a dialog with one or both of your parents, beginning with a question that you always wanted to ask, but never did or haven't yet.

❖ Describe the house or apartment and neighborhood or land you grew up in. If the place where you lived were an animal, vegetable, or mineral, what would it be and why? Finish this sentence: Growing up here was like . . .

❖ Describe your parents and your relationships with them. Write a story about each one that somehow captures what your relationship was like with each.

❖ Kohn left the farm for the city. Most children eventually leave home. What led you away from home or the type of life your parents led? Does anything lure you back?

❖ Write a story that somehow defines your relationship with the earth.

6

Genealogy and Genograms

Introduction

Why do narratives about our own relatives fascinate us more than stories about anonymous people? Why do family photographs and home videos command more attention than pictures and videos of unidentified strangers? Why is visiting a grave of a relative an experience often different from visiting a burial place of an unknown person? Feeling connected to our ancestors provides an awareness of belonging, of owning a past, and suggests that life influences go beyond our consciousness.

The forces that influence a person's life take shape long before birth. Memoir can thus transcend the day-to-day boundaries in which people usually think about their life. By learning about ancestors and by assigning significances to people and events that predate an individual's own physical existence, another fascinating dimension of memoir emerges.

The popular interest in genealogy manifests the belief of many people that ancestry and the influence of our predecessors do indeed matter in our life. Genealogy can be an invaluable tool for the memoirist. Howard Kohn, in his memoir *The Last Farmer*, ably demonstrates the fruits of genealogy by tracing his family farm back to his great-grandfather.[1]

The genogram provides a psychological tool to assist people in establishing and interpreting their place within their intergenerational families of origin. Memoirists have another useful tool in the genogram. The physical, intellectual, and spiritual dimensions of identity are revealed in the process and product of memoir, and tracing

134

one's lineage through genealogy and genogram can help a person understand determinants of identity and provide a route to freedom.

Genealogy Comes of Age

Assigning a specific explanation for the current widespread interest in genealogy is difficult. Certainly Alex Haley's 1976 book, *Roots*,[2] and the subsequent television miniseries rebroadcast often and available in video stores helped make genealogy a household word. The Church of Jesus Christ of Latter-day Saints, popularly known as the Mormon Church, has also contributed greatly to genealogical consciousness.[3] The church's highly regarded genealogical record keeping through their library in Salt Lake City, Utah, and its many satellite libraries and educational programs provide Mormons and non-Mormons with invaluable resources for learning about their own genealogy. The Mormons' computer software program Personal Ancestral File helps people to organize and manage genealogical information.

Other cultural trends also contribute to the widespread interest in genealogy. Among them are a renewed awareness of ethnicity, the mobile nature of our society, a growing multicultural consciousness, and new approaches to history. Descendants of immigrants who have journeyed back to family places of origin sometimes are perplexed to find that people there do not appear to share the same level of interest in genealogy. This might be because genealogy is all around them. Their ancestors are often buried in the cemetery next to their local church. Their homes might well have been in the family for generations. Attics and basements could be filled with forebears' momentos and memorabilia.

By comparison, few Americans live the village life of their ancestors. Americans move frequently. Americans have less immediate connection to places, and things that reflect family history and genealogical artifacts and information can be scarce. To create links to their own past, people without knowledge of their roots consciously need to seek out genealogical records.

Many immigrants surrendered their strong ethnic identity in favor of being "American." This was a common strategy for many immigrants and their children. Conformity was a highly valued avenue to success. What early generations close to the immigrant experience left behind as excess baggage, later generations set out to recover. A new consciousness has put aside the "melting pot" image of the United States and is gradually embracing diversity and multiculturalism.

New understandings of history have also given a boost to genealogy. Instead of relying on official sources of history, and focusing history only on what important people did, historians now look to many and varied sources. The common person's records are valuable resources for contemporary social historians. Many historians now hold diaries, journals, and letters of ordinary citizens in high esteem.

At one time genealogy was considered to belong exclusively to the realm of the aristocracy. Only important people needed to be concerned about their pedigree. Indeed, some people of rank thought little about falsifying their genealogies to alter their heritage, to eliminate a portion of their family's past that they considered detrimental, or to graft themselves into a bloodline valuable to them. Contemporary genealogy makes no distinctions between who should and who should not be concerned with their family history. Accuracy rather than fantasy motivates genealogists with integrity.

Genealogy may be open to everyone today, but the significance of specific genealogies may shift over generations. In Australia, for example, the significance of genealogy has taken some interesting twists since its colonial phase. When Australian identity centered on its colonial link to England, descendants of convicts, whose ancestors were shipped there as punishment, hesitated to reveal their genealogies. Today, just a few years after Australia's celebration of its bicentennial, claiming convict origins has become a badge of honor, not a symbol of disgrace. Australians able to demonstrate this linkage to the origins of their country were given special recognition by the government as part of the bicentennial celebration.

To the observant and sensitive reader of the Scriptures, genealogies are particularly intriguing. Matthew 1:1–17 and Luke 3:23–38 each include a genealogy of Christ. It is easy, of course, to skip over the litany of familiar and not-so-familiar names: Abraham, Isaac, David, or Aminadab, Nahshon, and Rehoboam. However, the genealogy in the Gospel of Matthew offers an important clue to Christ's revolutionary uniqueness.

This clue is found among the four women, in addition to Mary, in Christ's genealogy. Tamar disguised herself as a prostitute in order to seduce Judah; Rahab definitely was a prostitute; Ruth came from an alien land; and Bathsheba was seduced by David. These are not ordinary women. Christ's genealogy, as told in Matthew's Gospel, is not a traditional nor a prestigious genealogy, but Tamar, Rahab, Ruth, and Bathsheba "are included as examples of how unexpected, even scandalous, events are included in God's plan for Israel."[4] Like all genealogies, Christ's genealogy tells much about his role in history. Those who wrote his "memoir" understood this.

The Genogram Emerges

One contemporary tool by which the influences of genealogy can be traced is the genogram; it can also be a useful tool for the memoirist.

> A genogram is a format for drawing a family tree that records information about family members and their relationships over at least three generations. Genograms display family information graphically in a way that provides a quick gestalt of complex family patterns and a rich source of hypotheses about how a clinical problem may be connected to the family context and the evolution of both problem and context over time.[5]

Persons constructing a genogram are encouraged to include at least three generations on both sides of their family: two parents, four grandparents, eight great-grandparents. Add to that siblings alongside oneself and alongside parents of each generation, and the field of ancestors gets crowded. Add to that the contemporary phenomenon of second marriages and blended families, and some people's genograms become extraordinarily gangly. Since people have a lot of relatives, a lot of possible influences exist for anyone.

The genogram, developed by psychologists as a tool to aid in the therapeutic process, may, at times, seem deterministic. One reason may be that many people who come to therapy do so because of trauma. Hence, the development of the genogram in clinical settings, and its subsequent use, was generated in good part by problematic client issues.

If, however, the theory of the genogram is correct, then not only negative influences, but also positive influences can cross generational boundaries. The possible deterministic and negative connotations associated with the genogram become even less problematic when the concept of the genogram is broadened to include intellectual (thoughtlines) and spiritual (heartlines) influences. In addition to bloodlines and the dynamics into which each person is born, every person has the opportunity to make a choice of an intellectual and a spiritual genogram. Also, whether one is considering thoughtlines, bloodlines, or heartlines, personal and social dimensions further free the genogram from deterministic and negative exclusivity. These other arenas for the genogram's broadening dimensions open additional windows on the world of memoir.

Personal Bloodlines

Anyone who has delved into family history, either informally by listening to family stories or formally through genealogical research, is aware of numerous relatives, either living or dead. If all members of one's intergenerational families contribute equally to one's memoir, the end result becomes a blandly homogenized identity. No person is an emulsoid. Something else happens.

In an interview with William Least Heat-Moon, author of the best selling books *Blue Highways*[6] and *PrairyErth,*[7] I asked him what led him to use his Native American name rather than his European name. He told me that he used his Anglo name, William Trogdon, on the first several drafts of his first book *Blue Highways*. He elaborated:

> There was something wrong with the manuscript and some years into it, I realized what it was. What was really driving that book was that fractional part of me which is Osage. And the person writing *Blue Highways* was not simply William Trogdon. Yes, he was there too, but he was also Least Heat-Moon.[8]

So he rewrote the manuscript trying to listen more overtly, more consciously to "this other side." He explained:

> And it really was a return to the person I had been twenty years earlier. Twenty years in the academic world had not erased but had covered that over. I had forgotten those things. (They were also the twenty unhappiest years of my life.) So by remembering who I really was I made my own personal peace with the troubles I'd had. It's led me to where I am now. (11)

On the surface, using a Native American byline was a clever and effective marketing strategy, but something far more significant was at work. Bill Trogdon chose to reclaim and emphasize a physical and historical part of his identity and a part of his memoir. In doing so Heat-Moon diminished his European identity, another part of his memoir. Curious to know why a person might select a particular aspect of one's genealogy instead of another, I asked him if this was a voluntary choice on his part. Heat-Moon further focused the matter by calling it a conscious decision: "But I also happen to believe in, for want of a better phrase, genetic memory, in which we are inclined by the genes we have" (11).

He told me of an example from his own life. He had been fascinated for years with the work of stonemasons. "I almost got left behind by my tour in China in 1984 while watching stonemasons lay a wall. I could not take my eyes off what they were doing. It was a fascinating thing to encounter" (11). He found out about a year later that his great-grandfather was a stonemason on the Erie Canal.

> That explains the long fascination I've had with rock masonry. He is present. He also happens to be the only man I've found in my family who ever made a buck by writing. . . .
>
> So I did not choose that, that came; but now I choose, to use your term, to be aware of that and to develop it. So I think we are inclined, and I think once we learn our inclinations, then we can really begin to choose, to emphasize, certain inclinations. (11)

Of course this notion of genetic memory can be a dangerous idea. Racists, for example, can say that a particular race is genetically inclined to negative qualities and, therefore, should not be afforded rights and privileges that other races have.

Our conversation then turned to a consideration of the danger of genetic memory. Heat-Moon suggested that morality is a strong influence on how genetic memory might be used.

> Surely given all the ancestors that all of us have, we can each point to numerous criminals in our background. . . . But morality comes to play, too. You say: yes, I'm inclined that way perhaps by a long line of people thinking this or that about race, or religion, or politics or whatever, but I'm not going to act on those inclinations because I have a responsibility to choose, to make ethical choices. (11)

Social Bloodlines

Tracing bloodlines has social dimensions. Understanding this interaction can be a rich mine for a memoirist. For example, various national identities, like individual identities, exist at specific historical moments. National identities can change almost instantaneously or over a period of time. For instance, the central Asian republics of Kazakhstan, Uzbekistan, Turmenistan, Azerbaijan, Kyrgyzstan, and Tajikistan emerged as independent nations seemingly overnight. The ethnic identities of these new nations had been obscured by the nationalism of the old Soviet Union, but had continued to exist and re-emerged as a result of the overnight collapse of the Soviet Union.'

A slower, more subtle transformation of national identity is more usual for nations. The many lands invaded and conquered by various European countries once identified as colonies now exist as independent nations though the road to freedom was often long and torturous. Memoirists Jill Ker Conway and Richard Rodriguez both struggled with this social dimension of their personal histories.

What one thinks is authentic, real, and significant ethnic identity in the physical genogram sometimes breaks down under scrutiny. Take for example a narrative of Scot ethnic identity, an ethnicity I select because my own surname, Gilmour, is Scottish.

> The origins of most "people" are not known, but here and there we can find accounts of people-making activities that have taken place in the modern era. One historian, Hugh Trevor-Roper, has documented various inventions of the traditions that symbolize Scotland's distinct identity, all of which took place much more recently than most of us would imagine—after, not before, the union with England. Until late in the seventeenth century, the Scottish highlanders were not a distinct people but merely an overflow population from Ireland and linked to the Irish racially, culturally, and politically. The lowlands were populated by other racial groups including Picts and Saxons. Then there began a deliberate "cultural revolt" against Ireland, which combined a good deal of creativity with a good deal of plagiarism. Trevor-Roper credits the work of two men, James Macpherson and the Reverend John Macpherson (not related), who between them invented an ancient Celtic literature for Scotland and a history to go with it.[9]

The invention and development of ethnic and national identities today, as in the past, contain both possibilities and problems. The conflicts between Northern Ireland and the Republic of Ireland, the tragic events in Croatia and Bosnia and Herzegovina, and much of the bloodshed between warring peoples of Africa testify to the problematic nature of ethnic and national identities in a world striving for peace and harmony. The individual memoirist who examines his or her physical genogram with its ethnic and national aspects may offer worthwhile insight into these larger issues.

Personal Thoughtlines

For some people, the term *intellectual* carries heavy negative baggage, such as: vague, turgid, snobbish, effete, pompous, or aristocratic. When I use the term *intellectual,* I mean the appeal and influence of ideas as embodied in varied and diverse expressions of people that appears as uniquely human.[10] Knowing and reverencing ideas is not just necessary, it is good. To look at how each of us became educated is to look at a long process of ideas that touched our heart. To look at what each person finds interesting and what each person gravitates toward is to look at ideas that are part of one's intellectual genogram, one's thoughtlines. An intellectual genogram or tracing our thoughtlines can form the basis of fascinating memoir.

To become conscious of one's own intellectual influences, perhaps through the process of tracing one's thoughtlines, is in itself a fascinating concept and a task that leads to uncovering further dimensions of one's own identity. One person who effectively demonstrates the importance of raising to consciousness one's intellectual influences is Fritjof Capra. His book *Uncommon Wisdom* is an intellectual memoir.[11] He recalls and reflects on his world of ideas, how they entered his life, how he pursued them, and, ultimately, how they touched his heart.

Uncommon Wisdom also documents how institutions, particularly educational institutions, can at times constrict the boundaries of ideas. Capra's own intellectual journey involved a search for a new paradigm. He states, "A paradigm, for me, would mean the totality of thoughts, perceptions, and values that forms a particular vision of reality, a vision that is the basis of the way a society organizes itself."[12] The excessive compartmentalization of ideas in higher education that excludes interdisciplinary investigations alienated Capra from the academic arena: "I had already begun my search for the new paradigm and was not willing to give it up and accept the narrow confines of a full-time academic job."[13]

Capra's intellectual memoir draws an important conclusion— ideas do not exist outside of specific people and specific personalities.

He claims:

> The purpose of the book you are reading is not to present any
> new ideas, or to elaborate or modify the ideas presented in my
> previous books, but rather to tell the personal story behind the
> evolution of these ideas. It is the story of my encounters with
> many remarkable men and women who inspired me, helped me,
> and supported my search. . . . The stages of this intellectual
> journey and the meetings and conversations with the many re-
> markable men and women who shared with me their uncommon
> wisdom comprise the story of this book.[14]

Social Thoughtlines

In the not-too-distant past. the influences of the immediate culture or
society formed and focused a person's intellectual narrative. The notion of Western civilization is a highly influential, prescribed and pro-
scribed social complex of intellectual narratives. *The Great Books of
the Western World*, although heavily biased toward the social sciences,
canonizes selected ideas into an orderly, disciplined, lifelong curriculum.[15] Until the great curriculum meltdown of the late sixties and early seventies, there was much more basic agreement as to what best
constituted formal education. The interaction between society and
personal intellectual history can play a major part in memoir. For example, Heinz Kuehn's memoir, *Mixed Blessings,* reflects his exposure
to a classical curriculum.[16] *To Teach*, by William Ayers, dramatizes
how the vast changes in society have exploded the tidier intellectual
world of an earlier time.[17]

Long gone are the days when narrowly defined social or institu-
tional forces determined one's personal intellectual narrative. Today
many differing points of view influence a person's story. Contemporary memoirists interact with an enormous constellation of ideas that
influence their behavior, instruct their identity, and touch their heart.

Personal Heartlines

Spiritual memoir—memoir focused on one's heartlines—like physical
memoir and intellectual memoir, has both personal and social dimensions. However, the social influences of organized religions, which at
one time contributed mightily to spiritual identity, have ebbed. Other

factors often influence a person's spiritual quest and, ultimately, one's spiritual memoir, far more than organized religion.

Ethnic origin and geography hold less sway over spiritual heritage or heartlines than they once did. It is rare for people to be born, grow, marry, and die within a small geographical radius. Marriages involving people from widely differing ethnic groups coming from different spiritual traditions have replaced previously parochial matches. Spiritual traditions once bound by geography have been discovered and assimilated by persons outside of their specific cultures. For example, Native American spirituality now influences and attracts a worldwide cadre of people. Buddhism has flourished among westerners.

For many people, spirituality now stands apart from religion. People are now more likely to describe themselves as spiritual but not religious, at one time an unheard-of dichotomy. This phenomenon may both limit and expand the search for one's heartlines. Resources of religious traditions may go unnoticed, unappreciated, or unused in a person's quest for spiritual identity. The person who accepts the challenge to search for one's own spirituality cannot embrace one of the already developed, prepackaged spiritualities of a specific religious tradition. Nancy Mairs, in her memoir, *Ordinary Time,* embraces Catholicism while shaping her own spirituality that stands at odds with some official Catholic teachings.[18]

The search for spirituality outside of religious traditions can lead to the extremes articulated by Robert Bellah and others in their book *Habits of the Heart.*[19] Exclusively personal searches may generate so many individual "spiritualities" that a culture could end up with as many "religions" as people. Without a common spiritual bond, essential for a communal culture, rampant individualism gets inadvertently fostered and deified. "Sheilaism," as Bellah terms it, is the logical outcome of such a stance.

> Today religion in America is as private and diverse as New England colonial religion was public and unified. One person we interviewed has actually named her religion (she calls it her "faith") after herself. This suggests the logical possibility of over 220 million American religions, one for each of us. Sheila Larson is a young nurse who has received a good deal of therapy and who describes her faith as "Sheilaism." "I believe in God. I'm not a religious fanatic. I can't remember the last time I went to church. My faith has carried me a long way. It's Sheilaism. Just my own

little voice." Sheila's faith has some tenets beyond belief in God, though not many. In defining "my own Sheilaism," she said: "It's just try to love yourself and be gentle with yourself. You know, I guess, take care of each other. I think he would want us to take care of each other."[20]

Of course, even if people remain within the bounds of a specific religious tradition, there are often many styles and spiritualities from which to choose. Catholics, for instance, increasingly elect what parish or place of worship to attend based on style. One parish might have a contemporary liturgy, another parish might be more traditional; one parish might have an active religious education program, another parish might support a strong Catholic school. People also gravitate toward various spiritualities within a given tradition. In Roman Catholicism, people may gravitate toward Benedictine, Franciscan, Dominican, or Jesuit spirituality, to name just a few. More recently a specifically lay spirituality has emerged in Catholicism.

Social Heartlines

Spiritual traditions, old and new, do exist. They are embodied in memoirs named sacred by those who follow the originators of spiritual traditions. They are kept alive by people dedicated to the beliefs and activities of these spiritual progenitors. Spiritual visionaries whose memoirs have been named sacred and who have attracted a group of people dedicated to their beliefs and activities are significant social forces.

Certainly a person who consciously chooses to follow in the footsteps of a particular spiritual luminary finds that specific person in his or her heartlines. In the Christian tradition, all spiritual luminaries have Jesus Christ, the Jesus of history and the Christ of faith, included in their spiritual narrative, and the Jesus of the Gospels acknowledges the host of spiritual ancestors in his heartlines, recorded in the genealogy of the opening chapter of the Gospel of Matthew, in verses 1–17. Jesus was a Jew, rooted in the whole story of Abraham, Moses, David, and the prophets.

Christian spiritual narratives recognize their debt to their Jewish ancestors, the early disciples of Christ, the spiritual luminaries of historical Christianity, and to a vast array of twentieth-century believers, from Mother Teresa to Dorothy Day, from Reinhold Neibuhr to Billy

Graham, from José María Escriva de Balaguer to Daniel Berrigan, from Frederick Buechner to Mother Angelica, from Jim Wallis to Pat Robertson, from John Paul II to George Stallings Jr. All are spiritual siblings.

Conclusion

Every person is part of the great chain of being. Influences upon one's life existed well before each individual was born. These influences are both personal and social. A multitude of physical, intellectual, and spiritual narratives contribute to every individual's identity formation. Not ultimately determinant, but certainly influential, every person's genealogy and its subsequent genogram is fit material for the process and product of memoir. Such knowledge helps people to better understand the mystery of who they are and who they might become.

What ultimately attracts a person to emulate who and what characteristics they do, to choose one narrative over another, and, finally, to communicate one's own narrative through memoir remains profoundly intriguing. Equally intriguing is how memoir, by its nature personal, reveals the social nature of spirituality. Both William Least Heat-Moon and Fritjof Capra use the term "spiritual" to refer to wider worlds. Heat-Moon claims, "Any spiritual expression is an expression of some aspect of the imaginative life; that is, you can see beyond what's there in some way, you sense other existences, other forms of being. That's all dreamtime."[21] And Fritjof Capra, in a conversation with Stanislav Grof, claims, "Spirituality, or the human spirit, could be defined as the mode of consciousness in which we feel connected to the cosmos as a whole."[22]

Genealogy and the genogram are two windows on the social world that memoir embodies. They are also useful tools that memoirists may employ to mine the riches of life.

"All Rivers Run to the Sea": A Reflection

And yet.

Strange words to begin. An unusual phrase to conclude. More suitable *in medias res* as a transitional phrase. Elie Wiesel tells his readers "and yet" are his two favorite words. This man's exceptional lexical hoard could easily have led him to a love affair with more elegant words parlayed into a more eloquent phrase.

Here is a person who takes words seriously. Years ago when Elie Wiesel appeared at Loyola University of Chicago, cosponsored by Moriah Congregation of Glencoe, Illinois, he said, "One word is worth a thousand pictures." A few in the audience first thought he had the proverb backward, but by evening's end everyone knew he meant what he had said.

This recipient of the 1986 Nobel Peace Prize, the author of scores of literary works, and a tireless voice for the world's forgotten and persecuted offers a thousand pictures through each of his words in his memoir *All Rivers Run to the Sea* (New York: Alfred A. Knopf, 1995). He chides those who ask, "What's the hurry?" as he writes his memoirs. For him, this first of a planned two-volume memoir has little to do with his own age (sixty-six) and more to do with the Hebrew commandment *Zachor,* "remember." Since publishing his first book, *Night,* in 1958, Wiesel has followed this divine command.

> What does it mean to remember? It is to live in more than one world, to prevent the past from fading and to call upon the future to illuminate it. It is to revive fragments of existence, to rescue lost beings, to cast harsh light on faces and events, to drive back the sands that cover the surface of things, to combat oblivion and to reject death. (150)

He remembers particularly the Holocaust: its unspeakable events, the aftermath for its survivors, its perpetrators, the people who stood by, the people who helped, and all these people's children and their children's children.

At times the powerful words of Elie Wiesel, like those of Rabbi Mendel of Kotzk, remain silent even when written. He asks, "Is there a language that contains another silence, one shaped and deepened by the word?" (16). Wiesel remembers and testifies both with words and with silence. This memoir, like all of Wiesel's writings, is not cocktail party conversation.

As a boy growing up in the Hungarian village of Sighet, Elie Wiesel was more interested in the Hasidic tradition of Judaism than in sports. He spent long hours immersing himself in Jewish religious traditions through study, conversation, meditation, argumentation, prayer, and celebration. Along with two boyhood friends, Wiesel developed a fascination with the kabala, the study and practice of Jewish mystical sciences. Kabala, the tradition suggests, should be reserved for people over thirty years of age who are settled with wife and family. The kabala is not the stuff of childhood.

Here in the village of Sighet, Elie Wiesel, his family, and his neighbors first hear of Hitler's ongoing massacres. The facts were beyond belief, ignored until it was too late. One person who escaped an early deportation returns to tell his tale to unbelieving villagers.

Dazed, madness in his eyes, he told a hair-raising story: Those expelled (they were not yet called deportees) had been slaughtered and buried naked in ditches near Kolomyya, Stanislav, and Kamenets-Podolski. He talked on and on about the brutality of the killers, the agony of dying children, and the death of old people, but no one believed him. The Germans are human beings, people said, even if the Nazis aren't. The more convincing Moshe the beadle tried to be, the less seriously he was taken. He has suffered too much, people said, so much that he doesn't know what he's saying. Then he would lose his temper. "Listen to me!" he would shout. "I'm telling the truth, I swear it! On my life I swear it, and on yours! If I'm lying, how come I'm alone? Where is my wife and our children? What about the others, your former neighbors? Where are they? I'm telling you, they killed them. If you don't believe me, you're crazy." Poor guy, everyone said. Raving mad. Which only made him angrier: "You're irresponsible, I'm telling you! What happened to us will happen to you. If you want to look away, go ahead! But if I'm lying, why do I say Kaddish morning and night? And why do you say, 'Amen'?" That much was true. He recited the prayer for the dead ten times in the morning and ten times in the evening, attending every service, rushing from synagogue to synagogue seeking a minyan so he could say another Kaddish, and yet another. But the people were deaf to his pleas. I liked him and often kept him company, but I, too, could not bring myself to believe him. I listened, staring into his feverish face as he described his torment, but my mind resisted. Galicia is not exactly the end of the world, I told myself. It's only a few hours from here. If what he's saying were true, we would have heard. (28–29)

Only forty-seven pages of this four hundred thirty-two-page memoir recall Wiesel's concentration camp experience that began 19 March 1944, when he, his family, and neighbors were herded away. His father's death shortly before liberation on 11 April 1945 plunges him into tearless depression. More than forty years later, as Elie Wiesel sat with his own son, Elisha, at the Nobel Prize awards ceremony, the president of the Nobel committee, Egil Aarvik, said, "'You were with your father when he passed away; it was the darkest hour of your life. And this is the most glorious. It is therefore fitting your own son be with you as you receive the highest distinction humanity can bestow upon one of its own'" (95). Elie Wiesel saw his son and his father standing together at this moment. His eyes filled with the tears he was unable to shed so long ago.

After liberation, Elie Wiesel settled in France as a stateless person. There he began living a life: studying the Talmud, traveling, dating, going to movies and concerts, and studying at the Sorbonne. He learned who had survived and who had perished in the Holocaust. He educated himself.

I was intrigued and stimulated by the intellectual and artistic ferment of Paris. Still working on my education, I was an insatiable patron of the library. Never have I read so much. I devoured the works of Malraux, Mauriac, Paul Valéry, Georges Bernanos, Ignazio Silone, and Roger Martin du Gard. I read everything by Camus (why did he submit to German censorship and agree to delete the chapter on Kafka from his *Myth of Sisyphus?*) and Sartre (couldn't he have waited until Liberation to have his *No Exit* performed?) and was fascinated by the break between them. I discovered de Beauvoir, Arthur Koestler, and William Faulkner; Cervantes and Miguel de Unamuno, and of course Kafka. I compared their questions to mine. Could one be holy outside religion? Was there a secular priesthood? Where did man's responsibility end and God's begin? Would existence be absurd without God? I needed to be guided, but François was nowhere to be found. Nor was Shushani. I went back to my manuscript on asceticism determined to finish it, but doubt assailed me. What was so urgent about that theme? (189)

Wiesel eventually became a journalist because of his commitment to the Jewish homeland. When the United Nations passed its resolution "granting Jews the right to a sovereign homeland" (157), he naively but earnestly offered his services to Haganah, an underground movement. "And that's how I became a journalist" (158), states Wiesel. Although Wiesel's profession was journalism for a good number of years, his vocation was to write.

To write is to plumb the unfathomable depths of being. Writing lies within the domain of mystery. The space between any two words is vaster than the distance between heaven and earth. To bridge it you must close your eyes and leap. A Hasidic tradition tells us that in the Torah the white spaces, too, are God-given. Ultimately, to write is an act of faith. (321)

This specific act of faith, Wiesel's memoir, has an extraordinarily wide embrace: from concentration camp liberation to the Six-Day War; from little-known local rebbes to the mysterious Talmudic scholar, Mordechai Shushani; from chance meetings with strangers to encounters with world famous theologians, among them Abraham Joshua Heschel and Dr. Saul Lieberman; from fellow stateless people to heads of state, among them Golda Meir and Jimmy Carter; from forgotten villages to world-class cities, including Paris and New York; from Palestine to Israel; from Jewish communities in Brooklyn to Jewish communities in the former Soviet Union.

The real charism of *All Rivers Run to the Sea* resides in Elie Wiesel's mind and spirit at work. The golden thread of this memoir, summed up in the words "and yet," connects a mystical discipline, an insatiable quest for knowledge, a questioning faith, and a boundless imagination. Wiesel's roots in Hasidism serve him well as he embraces a wider world, perhaps unconsciously imitating his maternal grandfather, who "maintained a perfect balance between his quest for the sacred and the exigencies of daily life" (41). For Elie Wiesel, "the exigencies of daily life" included the great works of philosophy and literature: "Profane works had displaced sacred texts on my desk. The Talmud was no longer my sole concern" (274).

His focus on questions and questioning extends to God in the section "God's Sufferings: A Commentary" that follows immediately after the chapter on his concentration camp experience. "The barbed-wire kingdom will forever remain an immense question mark on the scale of both humanity and its Creator. . . . Which side was he on?" (105). And his many novels testify to Wiesel's intriguing imagination. "In literature, Rebbe, certain things are true though they didn't happen, while others are not, even if they did" (275) he told the Rebbe of Wizhnitz when visiting Bnei Brak, considered to be the most religious suburb of what some call Israel's least religious city, Tel Aviv.

Wiesel starts down many avenues of thought, but always returns to "and yet." He explains:

> And yet. Those are my two favorite words, applicable to every situation, be it happy or bleak. The sun is rising? And yet it will set. A night of anguish? And yet it too, will pass. The important thing is to shun resignation, to refuse to wallow in sterile fatalism. That great pessimist King Solomon put it well: "The days come and the days go; one generation passeth away, and another generation cometh; but the earth abideth forever. The sun also riseth, and the sun goeth down. . . . What has been will be. . . ." Must we stop time, then, and the sun? Yes, sometimes we must try, even if it is for nothing. Sometimes we must try *because* it is for nothing. Precisely because death awaits us in the end, we must live fully. Precisely because an event seems devoid of meaning, we must give it one. Precisely because the future eludes us, we must create it. (16–17)

And yet.

"True North": A Reflection

Like friends reminiscing about mutual acquaintances, I often wondered, "Whatever happened to Jill Ker Conway?" Her initial memoir, *The Road From Coorain,* focusing on her first twenty-five years, revealed an inner journey of feminist Australian consciousness. It illuminated a fascinating land and its people by exploring relationships between geography and spirituality, between place and myth, between earth and faith.

I knew that Conway eventually became president of Smith College and, more recently, edited an anthology of women's autobiographies. But I yearned for details, the deep description, the extensive examination, the incisive insight that made her first memoir remarkable.

True North, Jill Ker Conway's memoir (New York: Alfred A. Knopf, 1994), relates the next seventeen years of her life, from her Australian departure to acceptance of the Smith College presidency. I assumed this book would be about her life in the United States. What a surprise to find that along with her graduate studies at Harvard, this memoir centers on her personal and professional life in Canada. Yes, I am one of those people she criticizes, and rightly so, who assumes "America" means the United States. Her corrective is more than technical geography. It is in keeping with one of her signature themes— the sense of place and the unique spirituality each particular location engenders.

Before Conway settled in Canada, she earned her doctorate at Harvard. Conway's strong sense of self, her appreciation of other people and peoples, and her own developed spirituality of place supplied a worthy and worthwhile context for her academic studies. Her perspective on and her behavior at Harvard are refreshing:

> All my life in Australia, I'd been a solitary person studying late, going to bed in a darkened world, itself a commentary on my idiosyncratic interest in learning. Here, I was part of a community where everyone was awake, as intent as I was on mastering knowledge. It wasn't until I'd seen these images of a community engaged in a quest for knowledge that I realized how lonely I had been in Sydney. Here, I might be a stranger, knowing only a few charming people, and I might not yet comprehend many

aspects of the culture, but in a profound sense, I knew I belonged in this country of low slanting sunlight and blazing lights at midnight. We might worship the sun in the antipodes, but never this incandescence of the mind. (24)

Jill Ker's Harvard years were, in part, guided by faculty member Paul Buck who advised her to stay away from the big names when selecting courses since their ideas were readily available in their published works. He counseled her to choose instead the rising young stars whose ideas would shape the future. She followed his advice and also stayed away from other traditional treadmills of academia. She and her female student colleagues with whom she shared a house eschewed the elitism of Harvard. As she explains:

[We] didn't care for the treatment of knowledge as property. We lent our notes to potential competitors, shared new insights produced by our research, and, sitting in the comfort of our shabby kitchen, and still shabbier dining room, we denounced the intellectual habits of our fellow students who saw everyone as a potential rival." (44)

Other experiences broadened her Harvard education. When she met John Conway, her future husband, at an interview for a teaching fellow position in the general education program, she was impressed with his educational vision. "I'd come prepared to be very businesslike, to demonstrate my suitability for a teaching job, but it soon became clear that this man was uninterested in anything so graceless as a credential" (49). Her vision of education—community over institution, cooperation over competition, integrity over credential—motivated her to reflect years later on her reaction to the business of some academic committee meetings: "How many minutes of a chemistry experiment were the equivalent of learning to conjugate six French or Russian verbs? I couldn't care less about such silliness. It was the total conspectus of a student's experience that mattered" (247).

Throughout her time at Harvard, Conway was painfully aware of the lack of status and opportunity for women within those hallowed halls made hollow by such traditions. The position of resident tutor in the Harvard Houses was not open to women. Nor could even the most promising female scholar ever expect to be hired at Harvard after completing her degree there. This memoir testifies to the waste of talent by cultures and organizations that exclude or even marginalize women—or any other group—from full participation in their activities and enterprises. How many other potential Jill Ker Conways have gone unnoticed, unrecognized, uninvolved because of prejudice masked as tradition?

Her marriage to John Conway, toward the end of her student days at Harvard, shifted her status "from being a lowly graduate student, defined by my Widener [library] stall and the progress of my thesis, to someone who addressed all Harvard's luminaries by their first names" (81). And their almost year-long honeymoon in England and then Rome gave them an idyllic time away, save for Jill's completion of her dissertation and her husband's occasional episodes of a chronic depressive condition.

After the European sojourn, they settled in Toronto at a time when Canadian higher education was undergoing burgeoning growth and a change of consciousness. As Conway writes, "For almost the first century of the existence of higher education in English Canada, its purpose was not to plumb the Canadian experience, but to shape the Canadian identity by the rigor and energy with which British culture was explored and transmitted" (111).

Conway's adjustment, slow by her own admission, was another testimony to her sense of spirituality of place:

> The city was harder to "see" than most, because its charms were mostly private, and its distinctive mood and culture deceptively complex and different from the other English-speaking societies I knew. The cars were large, and American in style. The same supermarkets and fast-food stores cluttered the landscape. But these visual similarities to the United States were misleading. There were the same Midwestern lumber, grain, and industrial fortunes, but there was a world of politics, art, and literature I had to understand before I could register the visual and social cues of this society correctly. It was a fortress culture, slow to reveal itself, and I, at first, was too impatient a student. (124–125)

Her gradual love affair with Toronto "began to assume distinctive contours, no longer a shapeless unknown territory. . . . In museums and galleries I discovered evidence of a sense of the northern landscape, as powerful and mystical as any of my feelings about the Australian landscape" (135). Her visits back to her native Australia, although laden with her mother's needy personality, gave perspective to her now Canadian home. To arrive physically in a new land was easy; spiritual arrival was more challenging:

> Very slowly, almost imperceptibly, all my five senses readjusted to the Northern Hemisphere, so that its sights and sounds, progressions of seasons, flora and fauna came to play as vivid a part in my imagination and in the renewal of flesh and spirit as those of my native Australia. In part, the process was political, a gradual, but profound, transfer of allegiance to a political and social system I came to regard as fairer, more enlightened, more civilized than the Australian. But the sense of nature lies at the ground of our being because it shows us the forces of life by which we are sustained, and demonstrates, more powerfully than any other set of images, the potential for renewal and rebirth in living things. (167)

So the process of setting down psychic roots in a new country and drawing spiritual sustenance from the variety and wonder of creation was a process of reordering the imagination, imprinting new images, fusing them with deep impulses and values, so that they became the inner climate of the mind. She painfully realized the totality of her enculturation in Canada when she left to assume the presidency of Smith College in the United States.

Jill Ker Conway's voice is unique. Yet, at one point in her student career, she nearly surrendered it. As she worked on her dissertation, she momentarily lost her zest for writing until she realized, much later, "I had internalized the critical voice of the Harvard graduate student, and such a concern for theoretical rigor that theory got in the way of letting my imagination engage with my story" (91). As historian of her own life, Conway's academic training and talent are brought to bear in these memoirs, gloriously unfettered by academic voice:

> An historian who is a diligent biographer sees a life in the round, from many perspectives—associates, friends, enemies, family; from intimate records of inner life to public pronouncements. Soon the handwriting is as familiar as one's own, the characteristic habit of speech leaps from many different texts to proclaim the author, the faded photographs evoke the rich, full context of a life in all its contradictions, and the memories of friends seem like the researcher's own—memories of an intimate acquaintance. (65)

Now that Jill Ker Conway has detailed two major segments of her life, I wait for the next segment of her fascinating saga. Her next memoir, I hope, will center on her presidential years at Smith College. I suspect readers will continue to experience further insight into her sense of place, her vision of education, and her feminist conscious-ness. I'll be first in line to purchase what Jill Ker Conway already has lived but, as of yet, has not put into words.

Reflective Exercises

❖ Construct your genealogy back as far as you can go. If you know where your ancestors lived, what they did, when they lived, add these details. If your family has published a genealogy, study it. Find out as much as you can about your ancestors.

❖ Construct a physical genogram (bloodlines): that is, trace the ethnic, national, and cultural origins of your ancestors. Write stories that you remember grandparents, aunts, uncles, cousins, parents telling you that reflect this ethnic, national, or cultural heritage. Then ponder: How has my heritage influenced me? What attitudes come from my ethnic or national origins?

❖ Do what Fritjof Capra does in his intellectual memoir: Trace your thoughtlines, the ideas that have made you who you are. How did these ideas enter your life? How have you pursued them? How have they touched your heart?

❖ Write the story of your present spiritual journey. Where have you looked for direction? What key values and beliefs root your faith? What role has organized religion played in shaping your spirituality? Recall and describe key moments in your "religious history" that are still influencing your life.

❖ Moving often forces people to make all sorts of adjustments. What moves—to a new city, a new job, a new school, a new house or apartment—have been formative in your life?

❖ Write a story that somehow captures for you what it means to be a citizen of the country from which you come. If you live in a new country, tell a story about how you have had to adjust and redefine your life in the new place.

❖ Jill Ker Conway almost lost her "voice" at Harvard. Have you ever had a like experience in which the environment stifled or distorted what you knew to be your true self?

❖ Write about the biggest challenge you face right now. What is the most difficult decision that you have had to make or need to make? How has your past prepared you for and led you to the challenge and the decision? What about your past will help you meet the challenge and make the decision? What will hamper you?

Epilogue

I return to my colleague's question posed in the introduction: "Is it the fashion now to speak so personally?" My one-word answer, "Yes," was a good one for that particular moment; now at the conclusion of this book, the question has been answered more fully. Today many people speak and write personally in a multitude of settings. They communicate through narrative. They are, perhaps unwittingly, postmodernists.

The Quest for Stories

Tell me a story.

This perennial appeal by people across time and cultures is a uniquely human activity instinctual to the species. Little kids frequently get right at it in these exact four words as they climb up next to a parent, teacher, or friend. They might bring a favorite book they want read to them. Or they might want to hear an oral story.

Adults oftentimes are more subtle in their search for stories. They elicit stories in a variety of ways. "What ever happened to . . . ?" "What have you heard from . . . ?" Conversational questions trigger stories. Adults also search out other stories: browsing in a bookstore, library, or video store, channel surfing at home, meeting friends in a local coffeehouse, tavern, or restaurant. Like children, they long for stories.

The Quest for Memoir

Tell me your story.

This request focuses specifically on the personal. No longer is the story sought about someone else. "How was your day?" is an initial question triggering another person's story. Other situations and opportunities emerge for people to relate at levels of more depth. A curious, sympathetic listening audience facilitates the process.

People want to hear the incredible depth and breadth of experience within others, especially those people they admire and love. Story becomes memoir.

The Quest to Participate

I want to tell you my story.

The teller becomes the subject of the story as well as the author. Memoir, ultimately, is a participatory event. It is hard to keep silent, to remain uninvolved, especially in the company of personal stories. The process of one person telling a story from his or her life triggers other life stories from those who listen.

The specific vantage point each person brings to a given subject through memoir is unique. Like snowflakes, no two people's perceptions are exactly alike. One person's experience and vision might be close to or, at times, almost identical to another person's viewpoint. But experience and vision are never exactly duplicated. That is why knowledge and wisdom increase when people speak personally after serious and substantial reflection. Memoir contributes to the ever increasing pool of knowledge and wisdom by which we, as well as future generations, might guide our life.

From hearing stories to telling stories, from hearing personal stories to telling personal stories, this process replicates itself time and time again throughout every age and culture. Something vital is afoot here. Just as stories are a human activity, so too the stories we choose to tell make us who we are. They carve out identity in striking ways. They are crucibles for what people make sacred and hold sacred.

Expanding Horizons for Memoir

Today we have developed the education and interest for many more people to contribute their unique knowledge to the commonweal than ever before allowed or imagined. Yet work remains undone. We need to generate more interest in this genre of expression I call memoir. We need to make education more available. We need to extend interest in memoir to all segments of all societies, so that everyone's unique insights contribute to humanity's storehouse of wisdom. This is the stuff of spirituality; this is what religion needs to be more about.

This Book's Specific Memoirs

The memoirs reflected upon in this volume give a good indication of the far-ranging and far-reaching participation: an Australian outback girl who finds her way to womanhood through study at Harvard University; a thirty-six-year-old man whose brush with an often fatal form of cancer gives him new vision; a renowned South American writer whose only daughter dies after a year-long illness; a Mexican American who rejects the contemporary political rhetoric embodied in the term *Hispanic;* a woman who is feminist, Catholic, and fulfilled; an African American, born and raised in poverty, who receives his doctorate from the University of Chicago; a young man who comes of military age in Nazi Germany; a teacher whose journey in public education leads him to offer a spirituality of education; a woman who, somewhat surprised, enjoys her eighth decade of life; a journalist who, after happily leaving his rural home as a youth, returns when the family farm becomes endangered; a concentration camp survivor who attempts to find meaning in life; and a woman from Australia, the girl from Coorain, who becomes president of Smith College, a major United States college for women.

My reflections on other people's memoirs reflect my own life as a middle-aged American interested both in letters and in religion on personal and professional levels. Such is the experience of passing over, immersing oneself in another's life experiences, which leads to insights into one's own day-to-day life and lifestyle. This is especially true, I find, when a given memoir is vastly different from one's own life.

Creating Sacred Texts and Making Texts Sacred

These texts, then, like all authentic contemporary memoir and like the Wisdom Books of the Bible, are sacred texts. They capture and communicate something of the divine presence in the day-to-day activities of living and in life itself. They are theological reflection and a form of theology.

Like anything that captures, explores, and communicates the holy, stories themselves become sacred. Stories of other people's lives, as well as stories of one's own life, are sacred. Memoirs, then, stand alongside cathedrals as extraordinary sacred spaces capturing and communicating the presence of a God through artistic endeavor. Built of words and phrases rather than of stone and mortar, residing in psychic space rather than physical space, contemporary secular memoir attests to the presence of God in our midst much like the Gothic cathedral attested to the presence of God in medieval life.

> *Tell me a story.*
> *Tell me your story.*
> *I want to tell you my story.*

Notes

Notes for Introduction

1. Jill Ker Conway, *The Road from Coorain* (New York: Vintage Books, 1989).

2. Howard Kohn, *The Last Farmer* (New York: Harper and Row, 1989).

3. Lillian Schlissel, *Women's Diaries of the Westward Journey* (New York: Schocken Books, 1982).

4. Tim McLaurin, *Keeper of the Moon* (New York: W. W. Norton and Company, 1991).

5. Heinz R. Kuehn, *Mixed Blessings* (Athens, GA: University of Georgia Press, 1988).

6. Kathleen Norris, *Dakota: A Spiritual Geography* (Boston: Houghton Mifflin Company, 1993).

7. Brent Staples, *Parallel Time* (New York: Pantheon Books, 1994).

8. Doris Grumbach, *Extra Innings* (New York: W. W. Norton and Company, 1993).

9. Jill Ker Conway, *True North* (New York: Alfred A. Knopf, 1994).

10. Elie Wiesel, *Messengers of God* (New York: Simon and Schuster, 1976), xiv.

11. Nancy Mairs, *Ordinary Time* (Boston: Beacon Press, 1993).

12. See for example Roy Schafer, *Retelling a Life: Narration and Dialogue in Psychoanalysis* (New York: Basic Books, 1992).

13. See for example Malcolm Knowles, *The Making of an Adult Educator* (San Francisco: Jossey Bass, 1989).

14. William J. Ayers, *To Teach: The Journey of a Teacher* (New York: Teachers College, Columbia University, 1993).

15. Richard Rodriguez, *Days of Obligation* (New York: Viking, 1992).

16. Martin Kramer, ed., *Middle Eastern Lives* (New York: Syracuse University Press, 1991), vii.

17. Philip Phenix, *Education and the Worship of God* (Philadelphia: Westminister Press, 1966), 19–21.

Notes for Chapter 1

1. *The Oxford English Dictionary,* 2nd edition., s.v. "memoir."

2. Ibid.

3. William Least Heat-Moon, *PrairyErth* (Boston: Houghton Mifflin Company, 1991).

4. Ibid., 334.

5. Ibid., 335.

6. John Tracy Ellis, *Catholic Bishops: A Memoir* (Wilmington, DE: Michael Glazier, 1983), 9.

7. John Heenan, *Not the Whole Truth* (London: Hodder and Stoughton, 1971).

8. Michael Ryan, *Secret Life: An Autobiography* (New York: Pantheon Books, 1995).

9. Carolyn See, *Dreaming: Hard Luck and Good Times in America* (New York: Random House, 1995).

10. Michiko Kakutani, "Confession Is Good for the Soul and the Sale," *New York Times,* Friday, 23 June 1995, sec. C, p. 30.

11. Frederick Buechner, *The Alphabet of Grace* (New York: Seabury Press, 1970).

12. *Brewer's Dictionary of Twentieth-Century Phrase and Fable* (Boston: Houghton Mifflin Company, 1991).

13. Margherita Guarducci, *Peter: The Rock on Which the Church Is Built* (Rev. Fabbrica di S. Pietro in Vaticano, 1977), 29–35.

14. Arthur Miller, *Death of a Salesman* (New York: Viking Press, 1979), 56.

15. Robert Latham, ed., *The Illustrated Pepys: Extracts from the Diary* (Berkeley, CA: University of California Press, 1978), 9.

16. Ibid., 11.

17. H. R. Haldeman, *The Haldeman Diaries: Inside the Nixon White House* (New York: G. P. Putnam's, 1994).

18. John Ehrlichman, "Some Missing Pieces," *Parade,* 5 February 1995, 5.

19. John Tracy Ellis, *The Life of James Cardinal Gibbons, Archbishop of Baltimore, 1834–1921* (Milwaukee: Bruce Publishing Company, 1952).

20. Nelson J. Callahan, "Pluralism in the Nineteenth-Century American Church: One Perspective" (unpublished paper), 21

21. Ibid., 71.

22. John Bakeless, introduction to *The Journals of Lewis and Clark: A New Selection* (New York: New American Library, 1964), x.

23. Sherman Paul, introduction to *Walden, and Civil Disobedience,* by Henry David Thoreau, edited with an introduction by Sherman Paul (Boston: Houghton Mifflin Company, 1960), xli.

24. Robert D. Richardson Jr., *Henry Thoreau: A Life of the Mind* (Berkeley, CA: University of California Press, 1986).

25. Bradford Torrey, ed., *The Writings of Henry David Thoreau, Journal VI* (Boston: Houghton Mifflin and Company, 1906), 236–237.

26. Ralph Waldo Emerson, *The Portable Emerson* (New York: Viking Press, 1946), 568.

27. Lillian Schlissel, *Women's Diaries of the Westward Journey* (New York: Schocken Books, 1982).

28. Martin Luther King Jr., *Letter from a Birmingham City Jail* (San Francisco: HarperSanFrancisco, 1994).

29. Letter from Sarah Campbell to her parents, 6 August 1854, cited in Stephen C. Gilmour, *John and Mary Lunny Campbell and Their Descendants* (Sparta, WI: Joy Reisinger, Publisher, 1986), 53–54.

30. Stanislas de Quercize, cited in Genevieve Buck, "Finer Points of Pens' Popularity," *Chicago Tribune,* 21 August 1995, sec. 4, pp. 1 and 4.

31. Least Heat-Moon, cited in Peter Gilmour, "The Heartland Interview: William Least Heat-Moon," *Heartland Journal* 37, March–April 1992, 10.

32. William J. Bennett, *The Book of Virtues* (New York: Simon and Schuster, 1993).

33. Bruce Chatwin, *The Songlines* (New York: Viking, 1987).

34. Ibid., 205.

35. Ira Progoff, *The Practice of Process Meditation* (New York: Dialogue House Library, 1980), 11.

36. John Henry Cardinal Newman, *Apologia Pro Vita Sua* (London: Oxford University Press, 1967).

37. Edmund White, *Genet: A Biography* (New York: Alfred A. Knopf, 1993), xvi.

38. Morris Dickstein, "Intimations of Mortality," review of *Skinned Alive,* by Edmund White, *New York Times Book Review,* 23 July 1995, 6.

39. Charles Dickens, *David Copperfield* (New York: Penguin Books, 1966), 49.

40. J. D. Salinger, *The Catcher in the Rye* (New York: Bantam Books, 1951), 1.

41. Toni Morrison, *Beloved* (New York: New American Library, 1987).

42. Toni Morrison, cited in William Zinsser, ed., *Inventing the Truth: The Art and Craft of Memoir* (Boston: Houghton Mifflin Company, 1987), 111.

43. Ibid., 112.

44. Ibid., 111.

45. Ibid.

46. Ibid., 113.

47. John Pilling, *Autobiography and Imagination* (London: Routledge and Kegan Paul, 1981), 2.

48. Ibid.

49. Elie Wiesel, *All Rivers Run to the Sea* (New York: Alfred A. Knopf, 1995), 15–16.

50. T. S. Eliot, *The Waste Land* (New York: Harcourt Brace Jovanovich, 1934).

51. Frederick Buechner, *Now and Then* (San Francisco: Harper and Row, 1983), 2.

Notes for Chapter 2

1. George Stroup, *The Promise of Narrative Theology* (Atlanta: John Knox Press, 1981).

2. John Neihardt, *Black Elk Speaks* (Lincoln, NE: University of Nebraska Press, 1961), 1. Contemporary critical scholarship on this book reveals that the text ignores Black Elk's subsequent conversion to Christianity and his leadership role of catechist. See for example *Black Elk: Holy Man of the Oglala,* by Michael F. Steltenkamp (Norman, OK: University of Oklahoma Press, 1993).

3. W. B. Yeats, cited in John Pilling, *Autobiography and Imagination: Studies in Self-Scrutiny* (London: Routledge and Kegan Paul, 1981), 4.

4. Thomas Berry, cited in Brian Swimme and Thomas Berry, *The Universe Story* (San Francisco: HarperSanFrancisco, 1992), 5.

5. G. K. Chesterton, cited in Langdon Elsbree, *The Rituals of Life: Patterns in Narratives* (New York: Kennikat Press, 1982), 14.

6. Kent Nerburn, *Neither Wolf nor Dog* (San Rafael, CA: New World Library, 1994).

7. Herman Hesse, *Magister Ludi* (New York: Bantam Books, 1969), 413–453.

8. Saint Augustine, *The Confessions of Saint Augustine* (Oxford: Oxford University Press, 1991).

9. Luke Salm, *The Work Is Yours* (Romeoville, IL: Christian Brothers Publications, 1989).

10. *The Roman Martyrology* (London: Burns and Oates, 1962).

11. Alban Butler, *Butler's Lives of the Saints* (New York: Kenedy, 1956).

12. Ira Progoff introduces the term "Journal Trustee" in his *Life-Study: Experiencing Creative Lives by the Intensive Journal Method* (New York: Dialogue House Library, 1983). I derive this term from his understanding and use.

13. Thomas J. Heffernan, *Sacred Biography: Saints and Their Biographers in the Middle Ages* (New York: Oxford University Press, 1988), 21.

14. Malcolm X, *The Autobiography of Malcolm X* (New York: Ballantine Books, 1973).

15. Isabel Allende, *The House of the Spirits* (New York: Alfred A. Knopf, 1985).

16. Isabel Allende, *Of Love and Shadows* (New York: Alfred A. Knopf, 1987).

17. Isabel Allende, *Eva Luna* (New York: Alfred A. Knopf, 1988).

18. Isabel Allende, *The Infinite Plan* (New York: HarperCollins, 1993).

19. Isabel Allende, *The Stories of Eva Luna* (New York: Atheneum, 1991).

Notes for Chapter 3

1. Saint Augustine, *The Confessions of Saint Augustine* (Oxford: Oxford University Press, 1991).

2. Malcolm X, *The Autobiography of Malcolm X* (New York: Ballantine Books, 1973).

3. Thomas Merton, *The Seven Storey Mountain* (New York: Harcourt, Brace and Company, 1948).

4. Dorothy Day, *The Long Loneliness* (New York: Harper, 1952).

5. Kathleen Norris, *Dakota: A Spiritual Geography* (Boston: Houghton Mifflin Company, 1993).

6. Patricia O'Connell Killen and John de Beer, *The Art of Theological Reflection* (New York: Crossroad, 1994), 154.

7. T. S. Eliot, *Murder in the Cathedral* (New York: Harcourt, Brace and World, 1935).

8. Ibid., 70.

9. Known as "Ketuvim" in the Hebrew Scriptures, this section consists of these books: Job, Psalms, Proverbs, Ecclesiastes, the Song of Songs, Ruth, Lamentations, Esther, Daniel, Ezra, Nehemiah, 1 Chronicles, and 2 Chronicles. "The Law" and "The Prophets" are the other sections of the Hebrew Scriptures.

10. Although these books are traditionally designated as Wisdom literature, many other books of the Bible have passages that are aligned with the Wisdom Tradition. The influence and presence of Wisdom literature extends beyond these officially designated books.

11. Other Christian Bibles recognize the Book of Wisdom and Ecclesiasticus as deuterocanonical.

12. R. B. Y. Scott, *The Anchor Bible: Proverbs and Ecclesiastes* (New York: Doubleday and Company, 1965), xvi.

13. Ibid.

14. See for example Elizabeth A. Johnson, *She Who Is: The Mystery of God in Feminist Theological Discourse* (New York: Crossroad, 1992).

15. Vincent J. Donovan, *The Church in the Midst of Creation* (Maryknoll, NY: Orbis Books, 1989), 115–119.

16. Mary Catherine Bateson, *Composing a Life* (New York: Penguin Books, 1989).

17. Carolyn G. Heilbrun, *Writing a Woman's Life* (New York: Ballantine Books, 1988). Linda Wagner-Martin, *Telling Women's Lives: The New Biography* (New Brunswick, NJ: Rutgers University Press, 1994).

18. Walter Truett Anderson, *Reality Isn't What It Used to Be* (San Francisco: Harper and Row, Publishers, 1990), 3.

19. Pauline Marie Rosenau, *Post-Modernism and the Social Sciences* (Princeton, NJ: Princeton University Press, 1992), ix.

20. Martin Marty, cited in David S. Toolan, "Of Many Things," *America* 165, no. 8, 28 September 1991.

21. Frederick Buechner, *The Sacred Journey* (San Francisco: Harper and Row, 1982), 1.

22. James W. McClendon Jr., *Biography as Theology: How Life Stories Can Remake Today's Theology* (Philadelphia: Trinity Press International, 1990), vi.

23. Edward Schillebeeckx, *Christ: The Sacrament of the Encounter with God* (New York: Sheed and Ward, 1963), 7–10.

24. *Constitution on the Sacred Liturgy (Sacrosanctum Concilium,* 1963) no. 61.

25. Schillebeeckx, *Christ,* cf. 10–13, 47–89.

26. Donovan, *Church in the Midst of Creation,* 61–82.

27. Ibid., 63.

28. Ibid., 63–64.

29. Ibid., 74.

30. Patricia O'Connell Killen, "The Grand Inquisitor Revisited," in Peter Gilmour and Patricia O'Connell Killen, eds., *Journeys in Ministry* (Chicago: Loyola University Press, 1989), 103.

31. James Hopewell, *Congregation* (Philadelphia: Fortress Press, 1987), 165.

32. Roland E. Murphy, *The Tree of Life* (New York: Doubleday, 1990), 126.

33. Ibid.

34. Ibid.

35. John D. Barbour, *Versions of Deconversion: Autobiography and the Loss of Faith* (Charlottesville, VA: University Press of Virginia, 1994), 2.

36. Robertson Davies, *The Cunning Man* (New York: Viking Press, 1994), 167.

37. See for example Alan Wardman, *Plutarch's Lives* (Berkeley, CA: University of California Press, 1974), xiii, for the difference between Plutarch's *Lives* and his *Parallel Lives.*

38. Saul Bellow, *Dangling Man* (New York: Vanguard Press, 1944).

39. Saul Bellow, *Humboldt's Gift* (New York: Viking Press, 1975).

Notes for Chapter 4

1. Kathleen Norris, *Dakota: A Spiritual Geography* (Boston: Houghton Mifflin Company, 1993).

2. Mikhail Gorbachev, *The August Coup* (New York: Harper-Collins, 1991).

3. Sally Morgan, *My Place* (Boston: Henry Holt, 1987).

4. Ken Carey, *Flat Rock Journal: A Day in the Ozark Mountains* (San Francisco: HarperSanFrancisco, 1994).

5. Richard Rodriguez, *Days of Obligation* (New York: Viking Press, 1992).

6. Robertson Davies, *World of Wonders* (New York: Penguin Books, 1975).

7. Alfred Kazin, "The Self as History," in *Telling Lives,* Marc Pachter, ed. (Washington, DC: New Republic Books, 1979), 85.

8. James W. Fowler, *Becoming Adult, Becoming Christian* (San Francisco: Harper and Row, 1984).

9. Davies, *World of Wonders,* 16.

10. Walt Whitman, *Leaves of Grass* (New York: Viking Press, 1959), 22.

11. Thomas H. Johnson, ed., *The Complete Poems of Emily Dickinson* (Boston: Little, Brown and Company, 1960), 534–535.

12. Elliot W. Eisner, "The Primacy of Experience and the Politics of Method," *Educational Researcher,* June/July 1988, 15.

13. Ross Talarico, *Hearts and Times: The Literature of Memory* (Chicago: Kairos Press, 1992).

14. Jon Nilson, "Doing Theology by Heart: John S. Dunne's Theological Method," *Theological Studies* 48, March 1987, 71–72.

15. Dayton Duncan, *Out West: An American Journey* (New York: Viking Penguin, 1988).

16. J. D. Salinger, *Nine Stories* (New York: Signet, 1954).

17. Jonathan Kozol, *Death at an Early Age* (New York: Houghton Mifflin, 1967).

18. Robert T. O'Gorman, *The Church That Was a School* (Washington, DC: Catholic Education Futures Project, 1987).

Notes for Chapter 5

1. For another point of view see Alvin Kernan, *The Death of Literature* (New Haven: Yale University Press, 1990).

2. *The Oxford English Dictionary,* 2nd edition, s.v. "canon."

3. Sophocles, *Oedipus Rex* (New York: Harcourt, Brace, 1949).

4. See particularly Elie Wiesel, *Night* (New York: Hill and Wang, 1960).

5. Mortimer J. Adler and Charles Van Doren, *How to Read a Book* (New York: Simon and Schuster, 1972).

6. Samuel Taylor Coleridge, *Biographia Literaria,* Volume II, (New York: Oxford University Press, 1969), 6.

7. E. M. Forster, *A Passage to India* (New York: Harcourt, Brace and Company, 1924).

8. Adolph Hitler, *Mein Kampf* (Boston: Houghton Mifflin, 1943).

9. Charles Manson, *Manson in His Own Words* (New York: Grove Press, 1986).

10. William Ayers, *To Teach: The Journey of a Teacher* (New York: Teachers College, Columbia University, 1993).

11. Ibid., 27.

12. Natalie Goldberg, *Writing Down the Bones* (Boston: Shambhala, 1986).

13. Christina Baldwin, *Life's Companion: Journal Writing as a Spiritual Quest* (New York: Bantam Books, 1990).

14. Goldberg, *Writing Down the Bones,* 8.

15. Baldwin, *Life's Companion,* 25.

16. Ibid., 29.

17. James P. Armstrong, "The Holistic Depth Psychology of Ira Progoff" (Ph.D. diss., Loyola University of Chicago, 1984), 2–3.

18. Ira Progoff, *At a Journal Workshop* (New York: Dialogue House Library, 1975).

19. Ira Progoff, *The Practice of Process Meditation* (New York: Dialogue House, 1980), 16.

20. Erving Polster, *Every Person's Life Is Worth a Novel* (New York: Norton, 1987).

21. Ibid., ix.

22. Ibid., ix–x.

23. Doris Grumbach, *Coming into the End Zone* (New York: W. W. Norton, 1991).

24. Howard Kohn, *Who Killed Karen Silkwood?* (New York: Summit Books, 1981).

Notes for Chapter 6

1. Howard Kohn, *The Last Farmer* (New York: Harper and Row, 1989).

2. Alex Haley, *Roots* (New York: Doubleday and Company, 1976).

3. The genealogical records assembled by the Mormans assist them in their religion's practice of baptizing the dead. This custom is not without its critics. Officials of the Jewish faith, for example, found this Morman practice particularly offensive, and in 1995, reached an agreement with the Church of Jesus Christ of the Latter-day Saints that curtailed their ritual practice of baptizing deceased Jews.

4. William G. Thompson, *Matthew's Story: Good News for Uncertain Times* (New York: Paulist Press, 1989), 58.

5. Monica McGoldrick and Randy Gerson, *Genograms in Family Assessment* (New York: W. W. Norton and Company, 1985), 1.

6. William Least Heat-Moon, *Blue Highways* (Boston: Little, Brown and Company, 1982).

7. William Least Heat-Moon, *PrairyErth* (Boston: Houghton Mifflin Company, 1991).

8. Peter Gilmour, "The Heartland Interview: William Least Heat-Moon," *The Heartland Journal* 37, March–April, 1992, 11.

9. Walter Truett Anderson, *Reality Isn't What It Used to Be* (San Francisco: Harper and Row, 1990), 108–109.

10. Although I am aware of some of the thinking and research in the area of animal consciousness, I am not ready to either definitively accept or reject their opinions.

11. Fritjof Capra, *Uncommon Wisdom* (New York: Bantam Books, 1988).

12. Ibid., 22.

13. Ibid., 35.

14. Ibid., 12, 15.

15. Robert Maynard Hutchins, ed., *The Great Books of the Western World* (Chicago: Encyclopaedia Brittannica in collaboration with the University of Chicago, 1952).

16. Heinz R. Kuehn, *Mixed Blessings* (Athens, GA: University of Georgia Press, 1988).

17. William Ayers, *To Teach: The Journey of a Teacher* (New York: Teachers College, Columbia University, 1993).

18. Nancy Mairs, *Ordinary Time* (Boston: Beacon Press, 1993).

19. Robert Bellah et al., *Habits of the Heart* (Berkeley, CA: University of California Press, 1985).

20. Ibid., 220–221.

21. Gilmour, "The Heartland Interview," 11.

22. Capra, *Uncommon Wisdom,* 109.

Selected Bibliography

The bibliography is divided into the following thematic sections:
- Theoretical Explorations of Memoir
- Writing Your Memoirs
- Theology of Memoir
- Biography
- Memoirs
- Books About Memoir
- Fictive Memoir

Theoretical Explorations of Memoir

Barbour, John D. *Versions of Deconversion*. Charlottesville, VA: University Press of Virginia, 1994. Narratives that relate the loss or change of faith are explored and analyzed from both literary and religious perspectives.

Bell, Susan Groag, and Marilyn Yalom, eds. *Revealing Lives*. Albany, NY: State University of New York Press, 1990. Fourteen essays about "the workings of gender in the lives of women—particular women." Most of the chapters are papers prepared for the 1986 conference "Autobiography and Biography: Gender, Text, and Context."

Dennett, Daniel C. *Consciousness Explained*. Boston: Little, Brown and Company, 1991. "This book presents a theory that is both empirical and philosophical," the author tells us in the prelude. He moves beyond the traditional model of consciousness, which he calls the Cartesian theater, to a multiple drafts model of consciousness.

Elsbree, Langdon. *The Rituals of Life: Patterns in Narratives*. New York: Kennikat Press, 1982. Archetypal actions in narratives such as the following are examined: establishing and consecrating a home, engaging in a contest, fighting a battle, taking a journey, enduring suffering, and pursuing consummation.

Folkenflik, Robert, ed. *The Culture of Autobiography*. Stanford, CA: Stanford University Press, 1993. These collected essays offer a fresh understanding of autobiography by seeing it as part of a social structure and a particular culture.

Gunn, Janet Varner. *Autobiography: Toward a Poetics of Experience*. Philadelphia: University of Pennsylvania Press, 1982. The autobiographical situation, composed of impulse, perspective, and response, is investigated in *Walden,* "Tintern Abbey," *Remembrance of Things Past,* Augustine's *Confessions,* and *Black Elk Speaks.*

Hodgson, John. *The Search for the Self.* Sheffield, England: Sheffield Academic Press, 1995. The subtitle, *Childhood in Autobiography and Fiction Since 1940,* nicely focuses the topic of this volume. Chapter 5, "The Influence of Religion," in part II investigates this topic through examples, including, though not limited to, Mary McCarthy's *Memories of a Catholic Girlhood* and James Agee's *Morning Watch.*

Kotre, John. *White Gloves.* New York: Free Press, 1995. *How We Create Ourselves Through Memory* is the subtitle and theme of this well-written book that redefines memory within the contexts of narrative, autobiography, and identity.

Kramer, Martin, ed. *Middle Eastern Lives.* Syracuse, NY: Syracuse University Press, 1991. Biography and self-narrative in the West and in the Middle East are compared and contrasted. The final chapter, "A Sampler of Biography and Self-Narrative," written by the editor, offers a plethora of titles unfamiliar to many westerners and available in English.

Linde, Charlotte. *Life Stories: The Creation of Coherence.* New York: Oxford University Press, 1993. The oral life story as told over time on many occasions is examined by focusing on the social practice of creation, exchange, and negotiation. It presents and analyzes linguistic structures of life stories as an integral part to understanding their meaning.

Pilling, John. *Autobiography and Imagination: Studies in Self-Scrutiny.* London: Routledge and Kegan Paul, 1981. Examines autobiography through chapters on Henry Adams, Henry James, William

Butler Yeats, Boris Pasternak, Michel Leiris, Jean-Paul Sartre, and Vladimir Nabokov. Excellent introduction and conclusion.

Witherell, Carol, and Nel Noddings, eds. *Stories Lives Tell*. New York: Teachers College, Columbia University, 1991. Subtitled *Narrative and Dialogue in Education,* this significant collection of scholarly articles is divided into three parts: (1) Narrative and Ways of Knowing and Caring, (2) Narrative and Notions of the Self and the Other, and (3) Narrative and Dialogue as a Paradigm for Teaching and Learning.

Writing Your Memoirs

Baldwin, Christina. *Life's Companion: Journal Writing as a Spiritual Quest*. New York: Bantam Books, 1990. A superb guide to journal keeping filled with useful exercises, inspirational quotes, and wonderful insights that not only provide techniques for writing a journal, but the inspiration to do so as well.

Goldberg, Natalie. *Writing Down the Bones*. Boston: Shambhala, 1986. This delightful, challenging, and useful book lives up to its subtitle *Freeing the Writer Within*. Goldberg's sequel, *Wild Mind* (New York: Bantam Books, 1990), is also worthwhile. It is subtitled *Living the Writer's Life*.

Guzie, Noreen Monroe, and Tad Guzie. *Journey to Self-Awareness*. New York: Paulist Press, 1994. This journal of the spirituality of daily life is a specific and practical guide to introspection. The book's striking calligraphy is inspirational.

Ledoux, Denis. *Turning Memories into Memoirs*. Lisbon Falls, ME: Soleil Press, 1993. This practical, step-by-step handbook effectively combines the qualities of detail and inspiration. This book is based on lifewriting workshops developed and given by the author.

Metzger, Deena. *Writing for Your Life: A Guide and Companion to the Inner Worlds*. San Francisco: HarperSanFrancisco, 1992. Stresses creativity and includes many practical exercises. Part 4 is intriguingly titled "Writing as a Spiritual Practice."

Rothman, Seymour. *Your Memoirs: Collecting Them for Fun and Posterity*. Jefferson, NC: McFarland and Company Publishers, 1987. A practical guide for the would-be memoir writer.

Wakefield, Dan. *The Story of Your Life*. Boston: Beacon Press, 1990. Focusing on writing one's spiritual autobiography, this book combines highly communicative theory with specific exercises. A brief reading list in spiritual autobiography is included.

Theology of Memoir

McClendon, James W. Jr. *Biography as Theology: How Life Stories Can Remake Today's Theology*. Philadelphia: Trinity Press International, 1990. This text is a contemporary classic. Even though the author eschews memoir as overly subjective and therefore close to worthless as theology, his examinations of Dag Hammarskjöld, Martin Luther King Jr., Clarence Leonard Jordan, and Charles Edward Ives are worthwhile, as are the first and seventh theoretical chapters.

McCoy, Marjorie Casebier, with Charles S. McCoy. *Frederick Buechner: Novelist and Theologian of the Lost and Found*. San Francisco: Harper and Row, Publishers, 1988. This book, through an examination of Buechner's fiction and nonfiction, pulls together his imaginative and analytical works nicely.

Biography

Heffernan, Thomas J. *Sacred Biography*. New York: Oxford University Press, 1988. This book, subtitled *Saints and Their Biographers in the Middle Ages*, critically examines the motivations, styles, and customs of creating saintly lives during this period of history.

Pachter, Marc, ed. *Telling Lives: The Biographer's Art*. Washington, DC: New Republic Books, 1979. This book is a collection of presentations from a symposium at the National Portrait Gallery of the Smithsonian Institution. Contributors are Leon Edel, Justin Kaplan, Alfred Kazin, Doris Kearns, Theodore Rosengarten, Barbara W. Tuchman, and Geoffrey Wolff. Note particularly Alfred Kazin's contribution, "The Self as History: Reflections on Autobiography."

Memoirs

Baker, Russell. *Growing Up*. New York: New American Library, 1983. With the help and hindrance of a strong mother, young Russell grows up, at times to his mother's chagrin.

————. *The Good Times*. New York: William Morrow and Company, 1989. This book continues the chronicle of Baker's life started in his first memoir, *Growing Up*. It focuses on his professional life as a journalist during the Truman, Eisenhower, and Kennedy years in the United States.

Buechner, Frederick. *The Sacred Journey: A Memoir of Early Days*. San Francisco: HarperSanFrancisco, 1991. Buechner claims at the beginning that all theology, like fiction, is at its heart autobiography. The author, a Presbyterian minister, avoids abstract theological discourse in favor of creating a communicative, colorful memoir.

————. *Now and Then: A Memoir of Vocation*. San Francisco: Harper SanFrancisco, 1991. This second volume of Buechner's ongoing memoirs is equally as engaging as his first.

Capra, Fritjof. *Uncommon Wisdom*. New York: Bantam Books, 1988. Best described as an intellectual memoir. The author relates the personal story of how he came into contact with many of the contemporary ideas that shape his life and the world's cultures.

Crawford, Evelyn, as told to Chris Walsh. *Over My Tracks: A Remarkable Life*. Ringwood, Victoria, Australia: Penguin Books, 1993. This life memoir of an Aboriginal woman, her roots within her own tribe and her wings with the settlers of Australia, brings together two opposite worlds effectively.

Dillard, Annie. *An American Childhood*. New York: Harper Collins, 1988. Dillard relates growing up in Pittsburgh, a typical American city, in the 1950s. Her eye for detail and mind for imagination, qualities of her other writings, are also apparent in this memoir.

Facey, Albert B. *A Fortunate Life*. Ringwood, Victoria, Australia: Penguin Books, 1981. In his eighties, the author reflects back on his life and writes a compelling story that has become a contemporary classic in Australia. His boyhood, especially, is anything but fortunate.

Gilmour, Peter, and Patricia O'Connell Killen, eds. *Journeys in Minis-try: Nine Memoirs from Around the World*. Chicago: Loyola University Press, 1989. This book gives voice to the experiences of people in ministry from such diverse places as Africa, American suburbia, Australia, Peru, Taiwan, and Vermont.

Horton, Miles. *The Long Haul*. New York: Anchor Books, 1990. This memoir gives the author an opportunity to look back on his eighty years of life. He founded and led for more than fifty years the Highlander Folk School in Tennessee where many social movements were nurtured.

Monette, Paul. *Borrowed Time: An AIDS Memoir*. New York: Avon Books, 1988. Monette tells the story of his partner's nineteen-month fatal struggle with AIDS, their relationship, the communities of people who supported and hindered them, and their sources of strength during the ordeal.

———. *Becoming a Man*. New York: Harcourt Brace Jovanovich, Publishers, 1992. This book tells of the author's struggles as a gay person, growing up closeted and coming out in adulthood.

Morgan, Sally. *My Place*. New York: Little, Brown and Company, 1993. More than a coming of age memoir where the author discovers she is Aboriginal, not Indian, as her family has brought her up to believe. This memoir also captures the story of her mother and her grandmother, an intergenerational testament.

Neihardt, John. *Black Elk Speaks*. Lincoln, NE: University of Nebraska Press, 1979. The life story of a Sioux Medicine Man who, in spite of his vision to see his people flourish, experienced the destruction of his tribe. Originally constructed during the Great Depression as part of the Works Progress Administration (WPA), this memoir became popular in the 1960s, and has remained so ever since.

Norris, Kathleen. *The Cloister Walk*. New York: Riverhead Books, 1996. In this book, the author's second memoir, Norris details her experiences participating in the world of the Benedictine monasteries and the insights they offer to contemporary American life. It is a fitting and memorable sequel to her first memoir.

———. *Dakota: A Spiritual Geography*. Boston: Houghton Mifflin Company, 1993. This immensely popular "word of mouth" book captures the love affair the author, herself a Protestant, has with the Roman Catholic Benedictine tradition that she found when she moved to Lemmon, South Dakota, more than twenty years ago. Her reflections on rural American life are honest, to the point, and loving.

Scot, Barbara J. *Prairie Reunion*. New York: Farrar, Straus and Giroux, 1995. On a return trip to rural Iowa at the age of fifty, Scot discovers the inner dynamics of the lives of her parents, relatives, and other community members. Her parents' separation, her dad's eventual suicide, the tight-knit community of the local Presbyterian church, and the populations that preceded them—both Anglo and Native—give other meanings to farm life as archetypically American.

Talarico, Ross. *Hearts and Times*. Chicago: Kairos Press, 1992. A collection of poems that capture and communicate the memoirs of illiterate people by a talented poet. He divides the stories into four sections: (1) romance, (2) initiations, (3) possessions, and (4) seclusions.

Tollifson, Joan. *Bare Bones Meditation: Waking Up from the Story of My Life*. New York: Bell Tower, 1996. This journey of consciousness from suburban life to the drug culture, from the sexual revolution of the 1960s to Buddhist practice documents this woman's embrace of herself.

Verghese, Abraham. *My Own Country*. New York: Vintage Books, 1995. The story of how an Indian medical doctor practicing in rural America becomes the local AIDS expert.

Wakefield, Dan. *Returning: A Spiritual Journey*. New York: Doubleday, 1988. This author, novelist, journalist, and screenwriter writes deeply and well about his own journey of life. He is also the author of *The Story of Your Life* (see description under "Writing Your Memoirs").

Wiesel, Elie. *Night*. New York: Avon Books, 1960. This memoir of a boy's survival and his father's death in concentration camps has become the archetypical memoir of the Holocaust to which all others are compared.

Books About Memoir

Bateson, Mary Catherine. *Composing a Life*. New York: Plume, 1990. Through the lives of five women—Johnetta Cole, Joan Erikson, Alice d'Entremont, Ellen Bassuk, and herself, the author identifies and examines patterns and themes in women's lives.

Heilbrun, Carolyn G. *Writing a Woman's Life*. New York: Ballantine Books, 1988. A highly readable theoretical book that makes the claim that many classic biographies and autobiographies of women have suppressed the truth of the female experience. Mystery readers will be delighted to know that this author also writes under the pen name of Amanda Cross.

Zinsser, William, ed. *Inventing the Truth*. Boston: Houghton Mifflin Company, 1987. Six memoirs on writing memoirs by, among others, Russell Baker, Annie Dillard, and Nobel Prize winner Toni Morrison. Subtitled *The Art and Craft of Memoir*, this book reveals the struggles and challenges that "professional" writers endure as they work to produce their texts.

Fictive Memoir

Lodge, David. *Therapy*. New York: Viking, 1995. Largely written in the form of a personal journal.

Roccasalvo, Joseph. *Portrait of a Woman*. San Francisco: Ignatius Press, 1995. Roccasalvo generously tells three stories within one. One of the stories is a fictive memoir written by a major personality in the story.

Shields, Carol. *The Stone Diaries*. New York: Penguin Books, 1993. This intergenerational, feminist novel is rich in wisdom, and emulates, as the title suggests, diary entries.

Acknowledgments *(continued)*

The excerpt on page 7 is by G. K. Chesterton.

The excerpt on page 14 is from *Messengers of God,* by Elie Wiesel (New York: Simon and Schuster, 1976), page xiv. Copyright © 1976 by Elirion Associates.

The excerpt on page 16 is from *Middle Eastern Lives,* edited by Martin Kramer (Syracuse, NY: Syracuse University Press, 1991), page vii. Copyright © 1991 by Syracuse University Press.

The excerpt on page 17 is from *Education and the Worship of God,* by Philip Phenix (Philadelphia: Westminister Press, 1966), page 20. Copyright © 1966 by W. L. Jenkins.

The excerpts on pages 20 and 113 are from *The Oxford English Dictionary,* 2nd edition, prepared by J. A. Simpson and E. S. C. Weiner (Oxford: Clarendon Press, 1989), pages 593–594 and 838. Copyright © 1989 by Oxford University Press.

The excerpts on pages 20 and 21 are from *PrairyErth,* by William Least Heat-Moon (Boston: Houghton Mifflin Company, 1991), pages 334 and 335. Copyright © 1991 by William Least Heat-Moon.

The excerpt on page 21 is from *Catholic Bishops: A Memoir,* by John Tracy Ellis (Wilmington, DE: Michael Glazie, 1983), page 9. Copyright © 1983 by John Tracy Ellis.

The excerpt on page 24 is from *Death of a Salesman,* by Arthur Miller (New York: Viking Press, 1979), page 56. Copyright © 1949, renewed 1977 by Arthur Miller.

The excerpts on pages 24 and 25 are from *The Illustrated Pepys: Extracts from the Diary,* edited by Robert Latham (Berkeley, CA: University of California Press, 1978), pages 9 and 11. Copyright © 1978 by the Master and Fellows and Scholars of Magdalene College, Cambridge; Mrs. William Matthews; and Mr. Robert Latham.

The excerpt on page 25 is from "Some Missing Pieces," *Parade,* by John Ehrlichman, 5 February 1995, page 5.

The excerpts on pages 25–26 and 26 are from "Pluralism in the Nineteenth Century American Church: One Perspective," by Nelson J. Callahan, (unpublished paper, photocopy), pages 21 and 71.

The excerpt on pages 26–27 is from *The Journals of Lewis and Clark: A New Selection,* with an introduction by John Bakeless (New York: New American Library, 1964), page x. Copyright © 1964 by John Bakeless.

The excerpt on page 27 by Sherman Paul is from *Walden, and Civil Disobedience,* by Henry David Thoreau, edited with an introduction by Sherman Paul (Boston: Houghton Mifflin Company, 1960), page xli. Copyright © 1957, 1960 by Sherman Paul.

The excerpt on pages 27–28 is from *The Writings of Henry David Thoreau, Journal VI,* edited by Bradford Torrey (Boston: Houghton Mifflin and Company, 1906), pages 236–237. Copyright © 1906 by Houghton, Mifflin and Company.

The excerpt on page 28 is from *The Portable Emerson,* selected and arranged with an introduction by Mark Van Doren (New York: Viking Press, 1946), page 568. Copyright © 1946 by Viking Press.

The excerpt on page 29 is from *John and Mary Lunny Campbell and Their Descendants,* by Stephen C. Gilmour (Sparta, WI: Joy Reisinger, Publisher, 1986), pages 53–54. Copyright © 1986 by Peter Gilmour.

The excerpt on page 30 is by Stanislas de Quercize, quoted by Genevieve Buck in "Finer Points of Pens' Popularity," *Chicago Tribune*, 21 August 1995, sec. 4, pages 1 and 4.

The excerpts on pages 30, 138, and 139 by William Least Heat-Moon are from "The Heartland Interview: William Least Heat-Moon," by Peter Gilmour, in *The Heartland Journal* 37 (March–April 1992), pages 10 and 11.

The excerpt on page 31 is from *The Songlines*, by Bruce Chatwin (New York: Viking Penguin, 1987), page 205. Copyright © 1987 by Bruce Chatwin. Used by permission of Viking Penquin, a division of Penquin Books USA.

The excerpts on pages 32 and 122 are from *The Practice of Process Meditation*, by Ira Progoff (New York: Dialogue House Library, 1980), pages 11 and 16. Copyright © 1980 by Ira Progoff.

The excerpt on page 33 is from *Genet: A Biography*, by Edmund White (New York: Alfred A. Knopf, 1993), page xvi. Copyright © 1993 by Edmund White.

The excerpt on page 33 is from "Intimations of Mortality," by Morris Dickstein, a book review of *Skinned Alive*, by Edmund White, *New York Times Book Review*, 23 July 1995, page 6.

The excerpt on page 33 is from *David Copperfield*, by Charles Dickens (New York: Penguin Books, 1966), page 49.

The excerpt on page 33 is from *The Catcher in the Rye*, by J. D. Salinger (Boston: Little, Brown and Company, 1951), page 1. Copyright © 1945, 1946, 1951 by J. D. Salinger.

The excerpts on pages 33 and 34 by Toni Morrison are from *Inventing the Truth*, edited by William Zinsser (Boston: Houghton Mifflin Company, 1987), pages 111, 112, 111, and 113, respectively. Copyright © 1987 by Book-of-the-Month Club.

The excerpts on page 34, by John Pilling and the poem by W. B. Yeats on page 46 are from *Autobiography and Imagination: Studies in Self-Scrutiny*, by John Pilling (London: Routledge and Kegan Paul, 1981), pages 2 and 4. Copyright © 1981 by John Pilling.

The excerpt on page 35 is from *All Rivers Run to the Sea: Memoirs*, by Elie Wiesel (New York: Alfred A. Knopf, 1995), pages 15–16. Copyright © 1995 by Alfred A. Knopf.

The excerpt on page 40 is from *Now and Then*, by Frederick Buechner (San Francisco: Harper and Row, Publishers, 1983), page 2. Copyright © 1983 by Frederick Buechner.

The excerpt on pages 45–46 is from *Black Elk Speaks*, by John Neihardt (Lincoln, NE: University of Nebraska Press, 1961), page 1. Copyright © 1932, 1959 by John G. Neihardt, copyright © 1961 by the University of Nebraska Press.

The excerpt on page 46 by Thomas Berry is from *The Universe Story*, by Brian Swimme and Thomas Berry (San Francisco: Harper, 1992), page 5. Copyright © 1992 by Brian Swimme.

The excerpt on page 46 by G. K. Chesterton is from *The Rituals of Life: Patterns in Narratives*, by Langdon Elsbree (Port Washington, NY: Kennikat Press, 1982), page 14. Copyright © 1982 by Kennikat Press.

The excerpt on page 51 is from *Sacred Biography*, by Thomas J. Heffernan (New York: Oxford University Press, 1988), page 21. Copyright © 1988 by Thomas J. Heffernan.

The excerpt on page 93 by Alfred Kazin is from "The Self as History," in *Telling Lives,* edited by Marc Pachter (Washington, DC: New Republic Books and the National Portrait Gallery, 1979), page 85. Copyright © 1979 by the Smithsonian Institution.

The excerpt on page 96 is from *World of Wonders,* by Robertson Davies (New York: Penguin Books, 1975), page 16. Copyright © 1975 by Robertson Davies.

The excerpt on page 96 is from *Leaves of Grass,* by Walt Whitman (Ann Arbor, MI: University Microfilms, 1969), page xi.

The poem on page 96 by Emily Dickinson is from *The Complete Poems of Emily Dickinson,* edited by Thomas H. Johnson (Boston: Little, Brown and Company, 1960), pages 534–535. Copyright © 1890, 1891, 1896 by Roberts Brothers; copyright © 1914, 1918, 1919, 1924, 1929, 1930, 1932, 1935, 1937, 1942 by Martha Dickinson Bianchi; copyright © 1951, 1955 by the President and Fellows of Harvard College; copyright © 1952 by Alfred Leete Hampson; copyright © 1957, 1958, 1960 by Mary L. Hampson. Used with permission of Little, Brown and Company.

The excerpt on page 96 is from "The Primacy of Experience and the Politics of Method," by Elliot W. Eisner, in *Educational Researcher* (June/July 1988), page 15.

The excerpt on pages 98–99 is from "Doing Theology by Heart: John S. Dunne's Theological Method," by Jon Nilson, in *Theological Studies* 48 (March 1987), pages 71–72.

The excerpt on page 117 is from *Biographia Literaria,* by Samuel Taylor Coleridge (New York: Oxford University Press, 1973), vol. II, page 6.

The poem on page 120 is from *To Teach: The Journey of a Teacher,* by William J. Ayers (New York: Teachers College, Columbia University, 1993), page 27. Copyright © 1993 by Teachers College, Columbia University. Used with permission of the publisher.

The excerpts on pages 121 and 122 are from *Life's Companion: Journal Writing as a Spiritual Quest,* by Christina Baldwin (New York: Bantam Books, 1990), pages 25 and 29. Copyright © 1990 by Christina Baldwin.

The excerpts on pages 122 and 123 are from *The Holistic Depth Psychology of Ira Progoff,* by James P. Armstrong (Ph.D. dissertation, Loyola University of Chicago, 1984), pages 2–3.

The excerpts on page 123 are from *Every Person's Life Is Worth a Novel,* by Erving Polster (New York: W. W. Norton and Company, 1987), pages ix and ix–x.

The excerpt on page 137 is from *Matthew's Story: Good News for Uncertain Times,* by William G. Thompson, SJ (New York: Paulist Press, 1989), page 58. Copyright © 1989 by the Detroit Province of the Society of Jesus.

The excerpt on page 137 is from *Genograms in Family Assessment,* by Monica McGoldrick and Randy Gerson (New York: W. W. Norton and Company, 1985), page 1. Copyright © 1985 by Monica McGoldrick and Randy Gerson.

The excerpts on pages 141, 142, and 145 are from *Uncommon Wisdom,* by Fritjof Capra (New York: Bantam Books, 1988), pages 22, 35, 12, 15, and 109, respectively. Copyright © 1988 by Fritjof Capra. Used with permission of Simon and Schuster.

The excerpts on pages 143–144 are from *Habits of the Heart,* by Robert Bellah et al. (Berkeley, CA: University of California Press, 1985), pages 220–221. Copyright © 1985 by the Regents of the University of California Press. Used with permission.

Acknowledgments for the reviews in the reflection sections

The excerpts on pages 36–39 are from *The Road from Coorain,* by Jill Ker Conway (New York: Vintage Books, 1990), pages 24–25, 69, 25, 5, 195, and 218–219, respectively. Copyright © 1989 by Jill Conway.

The excerpts on pages 40–42 are from *Keeper of the Moon,* by Tim McLaurin (New York: W. W. Norton and Company, 1991), pages 277, 32, 38, 275, and 316, respectively. Copyright © 1991 by Tim McLaurin.

The excerpts on pages 54–58 are from *Paula,* by Isabel Allende, translated by Margaret Sayers Peden (San Francisco: HarperCollins, Publishers, 1994), pages 313, 8, 170–171, 217–218, and 325, respectively. Copyright © 1994 by Isabel Allende, translation copyright © 1995 by HarperCollins Publishers.

The excerpts on pages 59–62 are from *Days of Obligation: An Argument with My Mexican Father,* by Richard Rodriguez (New York: Viking Penguin, 1992), pages 69–70, 122, 28, 130, 132, 20, 194, 195–196, xvi, 106, xviii, and 169, respectively. Copyright © 1992 by Richard Rodriguez.

The excerpts on pages 81–84 are from *Ordinary Time: Cycles in Marriage, Faith, and Renewal,* by Nancy Mairs (Boston: Beacon Press, 1993), pages 7, 11, 8, 206, 71, 86, 12, 168, 99, and 89, respectively. Copyright © 1993 by Nancy Mairs.

The excerpts on pages 85–89 are from *Parallel Time: Growing Up in Black and White,* by Brent Staples (New York: Pantheon Books, 1994), pages 11–12, 26, 32, 98, 31, 62, 58, 68, 72, 69, and 260, respectively. Copyright © 1994 by Brent Staples.

The excerpts on pages 101–105 are from *Mixed Blessings: An Almost Ordinary Life in Hitler's Germany,* by Heinz R. Kuehn (Athens, GA: University of Georgia Press, 1988), pages 169, 27–28, 10, 70, 22, and 104, respectively. Copyright © 1988 by the University of Georgia Press.

The excerpts on pages 106–110 are from *To Teach: The Journey of a Teacher,* by William J. Ayers (New York: Teachers College, Columbia University, 1993), pages ix, 18, 88, 32, 37, 39, 57, 114, 116, 119, 124, and 64–65, respectively. Copyright © 1993 by Teachers College, Columbia University.

The excerpts on pages 125–128 are from *Extra Innings: A Memoir,* by Doris Grumbach (New York: W. W. Norton and Company, 1993), pages 28, 40, 236, 9, 14–15, 71, 127, 33–34, 71, and 90, respectively. Copyright © 1993 by Doris Grumbach.

The excerpts on pages 129–131 are from *The Last Farmer: An American Memoir,* by Howard Kohn (New York: Harper and Row, Publishers, 1989), pages 17–18, 257, and 269–270, respectively. Copyright © 1988 by Howard Kohn.

The excerpts on pages 146–150 are from *All Rivers Run to the Sea: Memoirs,* by Elie Wiesel (New York: Alfred A. Knopf, 1995), pages 150, 16, 28–29, 95, 189, 157, 158, 321, 41, 274, 105, 275, and 16–17, respectively. Copyright © 1995 by Alfred A. Knopf.

The excerpts on pages 151–155 are from *True North: A Memoir,* by Jill Ker Conway (New York: Alfred A. Knopf, 1994), pages 24, 44, 49, 247, 81, 111, 124–125, 135, 167, 91, and 65, respectively. Copyright © 1994 by Jill Ker Conway.